"Find a need and fill it. Francis Miller has done an admirable job of doing precisely that. There are thousands of brokers but nobody has told you in simple and clearly understandable English how to choose a good one. Here Miller takes you by the hand and leads you step-by-step through the quest—not only how to bring this off—but describing in detail the entire relationship between broker and customer. He examines this broker-customer marriage from each side and then defines and examines the entire catalogue of basic knowledge that everybody should know about how the market operates. So, if you have a stock broker you need this book to see if he or she measures up. If you don't have a broker, good, you now don't have to ever have the bad experience of picking a poor one."

. . . . .Joseph E. Granville

SAVVY
INVESTORS

SAVVY INVESTORS

Francis W. Miller

Dunhill Publishing Company
New York

A DUNHILL TRADE PAPERBACK
Published by: Dunhill Publishing Co.
A division of the Zinn Publishing Group
ZINN COMMUNICATIONS / NEW YORK

ISBN: 0-935016-20-1

Printed in the United States of America

Library of Congress Cataloging-in-Publication Data

Miller, Francis W., 1946—
    Savvy Investors   :   choosing the right stockbroker for maximum profits / Francis W. Miller.
        p.   cm
    ISBN 0-935016-20-1 (pbk.)
    1.   Stockbrokers—United States. 2. Investments—United States.
    I.   Title.
    HG4928.5.M555   1997
    332.63'22—DC20   96-18822
                                                          CIP

To my wife Linda,
my family,
my fellow brokers,
and especially to,
my clients.

My thanks to you all.

Table of Contents

Acknowledgements

Most first time book authors, as I am, spend many arduous hours of labor in an effort that they can never be sure will be successful. Especially if, like me, they are working full time in order to provide for their families and themselves, those hours can be extremely hard to find. You have to love writing. You have to lean on the faith and confidence that your close family and friends have in you.

Most first time authors, after finishing their work (or thinking that they have) come to realize that the writing was the easy part. Fifty or a hundred thousand words are meaningless, unless someone somewhere, has enough faith in them to see that they are presented to the market for which they were intended.

A first time author does not have an agent. Nor does he have the publisher who will take the verbiage and incorporate it into its final book format, with a great title, a superior book cover and a format that will allow those words to flow freely to their intended audience. Even then, the work is meaningless without the marketing efforts of the publisher. The book world is, after all, a business.

My first thank you goes to David Zinn of Barclay House. David, you did an absolutely fantastic job on this book and even with your very busy schedule, you had the patience to put up with all of my often terribly naive questions. Thanks again.

No book is the effort of one person. The author may have the idea and may pen the words, but countless others must support the effort that will eventually lead to the final product.

If I had to thank only one person for the reality of this book, it would have to be Cynthia Sterling, my literary agent at the *Lee Shore Literary Agency*. Cynthia has an absolute passion for writing and she alone, was able to see in my original manuscript (the one I thought was perfect) the potential for a reasonably successful book. An author is nothing without a literary agent and for a first time author, finding the right one is no small feat. Cynthia had the faith in me that I desperately needed and when I would become frustrated, her few words of literary wisdom would see me through. Thank you Cynthia, for your faith, understanding, and expertise.

Along with Cynthia, I must thank her staff. All of them were extremely helpful, but none more than Megan Davidson, Cynthia's Editor-in-Chief. An editor's work is difficult. Megan was the one that ripped into my first manuscript. Together with Brenda, a staff editor, they "insulted" my original effort and in doing so, taught me far more about writing than I could have ever learned in a classroom. The result was a far superior effort than was my first work. Thanks also, Megan, for your patience in answering all of my nuisance "first time author" questions!

Countless evenings, weekends and holidays were spent compiling and revising the verbiage that eventually became this book. My wife Linda and my sons Jim and Joey, did without a husband and a father for many a spare hour. For my sons, it was probably no big deal. They're older now, and they find their own avenues of endeavor without me. Non-the-less, they lost a father for many a spare hour and for their support, I thank them.

Anyone who is writing to be published for the first time,

can suffer a very severe lack of confidence. Is what I am saying really significant? Is it pertinent? Does it really have meaning or is it just literary garbage? There is no way to know—unless you can bounce it off of a really true friend who both knows what you're talking about, and also knows you well enough to tell you whether it's really good, or really rotten.

My very good friend Richard was and is, such a person to me. Having come originally from bank management, and having developed a very successful brokerage business of his own, he was instantly able to dissect my copy and give it to me straight. When I would write something that I felt was good—but lacked confidence in, I would throw it on Rich's desk. I would almost instantly get an answer.

"Frank, this is great. You really tell it like it is. You've got a way with words and this really needs to be said. I hope this publishes because people really need to know this."

"Frank, this is kind'a off the wall. I think you have to re-visit this part. How's about..."

I could always depend on Richard's in depth knowledge of the business, combined with a friendship which was strong enough to tell me how he really felt. If he liked it, he'd say so. If I was off track, he'd say that too. Thanks Rich. Your advice was invaluable.

I would also like to thank my two other close friends, Ray and Phil. They have both been close associates of mine. The ability to bounce my investment ideas off of each of them has helped me (and my clients) in ways that are immeasurable.

I owe depths of gratitude to other brokers in the industry. My lawyers suggest that I shouldn't mention them by name here, (their companies might take offense) but thanks guys and gals. You know who you are!

Ed Madden (now deceased) brought me into the business. He had the faith in me that I needed, and he nurtured me as I matured in the field. As my first manager, he helped me through both the difficult and the good times. Eddie, if you're looking down at me from where I know you must be, thanks—a thousand fold.

Two other managers welcomed me into their offices and provided both me and my clients a comfortable and very positive environment in which to do business. I and my clients thank Kevin and Jeff for their continued support -- and speaking of clients, I also owe them my thanks. I have both taught them and learned from them. We've had great times and more than a few laughs together.

My parents instilled in me the ethics that have endured throughout my lifetime. Even as a soldier in Vietnam, when at times I thought I would never return, and the rules for survival were far different than those we know in America, their principals of simple honesty and integrity were with me. (As the father of my own sons now, I know how you must have worried for me back then—but hey! I made it!)

My late father-in-law, Ben Rabiola, taught me perseverance and dedication. As a highly skilled craftsman, he demonstrated the pride we can take in knowing we have given our best. My mother-in-law Josephine, taught me wisdom. Her constant insight and concern for other people, showed me the importance of truly caring for people, their individual needs, and their concerns.

My father's cousin and my second cousin, Colonel Bud Schuman was always a driving force in my life. He coached me through the military service. He was my first (and is still one of my best) clients. He is in fact, my second father. Whenever I have a question or problem that's a little too sensitive or intimate for the immediate family, "Cousin Buddy's" the one I can turn to.

I couldn't possibly close these acknowledgements without thanking my lovely wife Linda. Countless hours were spent by her, without her spouse, while I was concocting this book. No single person in the world knows me better than she. No single person in the world means more to me, than Linda.

While she may have had doubts about this book (after all, I had spent countless previous hours writing a novel that never quite made it), Linda never lost faith in me. She has always loved and stood by me. Without her patience, understanding and perseverance, this book—simply would have been impossible. Few men have been as fortunate as I, to have shared life with such a wonderful woman. Still luv ya' kid, even after all these years!

To all of you, and to all of my readers,

I hope you enjoy the book
as much as I did writing it.

Who is the
Modern Broker?

1

Who is the modern Stock Broker?

There are just under ninety three thousand registered investment brokers working today in the United States. At a conservative estimate of two hundred clients per broker, they have about nineteen million clients. Let's assume a few people have more than one broker. Let's assume a few brokers have more than two hundred clients. Maybe clients only number fifteen million or so. Regardless of exactly how many clients there are, I would guess that less than one percent of them have an inkling as to how the broker does business. Who is it you, the client are working with? What are your broker's priorities? What are his frustrations? How does his business really work? Who are the clients? Are clients the bosses or the pawns in this relationship? Is the broker merely the pawn? What misconceptions do you have about your brokers? What kind of broker do you have? What kind of client are you?

Brokers today come with many different titles. There are so many titles that try to either describe or deceive clients as to the function of a broker that, for purposes of brevity, we are going to refer to this unique individual for now, simply as a "broker."

Whether one is called a financial consultant, investment broker, financial broker, financial advisor, customer's man or vice president of investments, if he is a broker, his objective is always the same. He invests or "places" your money for you. He buys you investment securities, earning a commission as he does so.

Most clients have no idea how a title is conferred on a broker. One might be led to believe that the title of Vice President or Senior Broker would insinuate competence and expertise. Not so. It's strictly an indication of how much commission or "production" the broker can generate. The more a broker makes in commissions, the more grandiose his title. In the brokerage industry promotions do not include additional compensation. Brokers are not recognized for how much money they make their clients. They are recognized for how much commission they earn for themselves and their companies.

When you are selecting or dealing with a broker, you really shouldn't concern yourself too much with the title he wears. A ruthless broker in the business for only two years could easily become a vice president. He'll do anything to grab a commission, whether it's good or bad for his clients. On the other hand, a ten-year-veteran that's only a financial consultant might be operating with his client's best interests as his major concern, and he may be foregoing a lot of commission dollar in the process. Which one of these fellows do you want as your broker?

The generally accepted definition of a broker is a person that acts as an intermediary between the buyer and seller of a product. This person is usually, but not always, licensed by a government agency. The license supposedly offers proof that the broker has knowledge of what he is talking about. A real estate agent or broker, an auction broker, a food broker—all are intermediaries. An investment broker is no different.

The problem develops when brokerage companies start

re-naming these people purely for marketing purposes. They figure you may not want to deal with a stock broker, but a financial consultant might appeal to you even if it's the same person. Is a stock broker actually a financial consultant? Is a vice president of investments still a broker? All of these fancy terms sound impressive to clients, but they don't take away the fact that this person is still a broker.

Many people today, perhaps too many, still think of a stock broker in the age old stereotype.

"Have I got a stock for you!"
"Hey, wanna make some big money real fast?"
"You better buy now. This stock is going UP!"

These brokers still exist, but their numbers are rapidly dwindling. The modern day stock broker had to learn about far more than stocks just to pass the securities exam he took. His license required him to be proficient not only in stocks and options, but limited partnerships, mutual funds, bonds, taxes and many other aspects pertaining to the investment of funds in the current financial markets. We will see that various brokers choose to do their business in various ways and many still like a "hot stock" but in the modern day world you should expect your stock broker to be qualified to handle and explain just about any investment situation you might have.

This is the investment professional that you can talk to. He is universally referred to as a Registered Representative, generally referred to by any number of descriptive titles and most often referred to by his nickname of "stock broker". This is the broker you can call every day or every week, or maybe once a month or perhaps even less; the direct contact you have in the investment world to offer you ideas. He can review your holdings and your investment goals with you as no one else can. He already knows, or learns to know you personally. He knows the financial markets intimately and is licensed by the various regulators to place you directly into those markets. He is the match maker. Because he knows both you and the many investment opportunities available to you, he is uniquely qualified to perform the perfect marriage. He can find for you, the investments most perfectly fitting your needs, desires and requirements.

Why do modern investors use stock brokers? There are various relationships between clients and the professionals whose services they seek out. The relationship between stock broker and client is similar to the relationship with automobile mechanics.

Some people really love cars. They're serious hobbyists. They only go to the mechanic when they have a problem that's over their heads, or perhaps when they simply don't have the time to fix the car themselves. Others are shade tree mechanics. They will tinker with the little things. They may even occasionally take on a larger problem by themselves. They are not really good mechanics but they enjoy the tinkering. If they save a few dollars in the process that's okay too, but the big problems definitely go to the mechanic. Other people simply have no knowledge and no interest in the mysterious things that go on under the hood of their cars. They go to their mechanics for everything the car needs.

You might want to think of your stock broker as your financial mechanic. You probably haven't heard that one before but it sure works for me and I'm a stock broker.

You may be a hobbyist. You really know your stuff. You rarely need an investment broker but if the investment you just bought is quickly losing money and you need to know why in a hurry, you'll really need him!

You may like to dabble in the markets from time to time on your own, saving a little money in the process, but you know you have neither the time or the expertise to handle all of your investments without some help. You need the advice and ideas that the stock broker has at his disposal. It takes a lot of homework. A lot of reading. There's a lot of studying, analysis, and background detail work to be done, and constant follow up. The performance of an investment must be reviewed constantly. You need your stock broker.

You may not understand a thing that goes on under the hood of that car, or in the investment world. You definitely need your stock broker.

You also may not be capable of making required decisions due to your lack of investment knowledge. If you can't make intelligent investment decisions quickly and without hesitation, in today's brutally fast-moving investment environment, you absolutely, positively, without any doubt need your investment broker—big time! You must learn to trust in his ability to make those instantly required decisions for you.

"Okay," you are saying to yourself. "This Stock Broker thing looks like it could work for me, but these guys require me to have a whole lot of money. All I have is that forty thousand sitting in the CD. They won't talk to me."

Oh really? Don't worry, he'll talk to you. The brokerage industry also suffers from another stereotype seen in the old movies. Robber barons and their rich stock brokers. Millions of dollars at stake. Only for the really rich. Lots of dollars to play with.

Obviously this still happens. There are fortunes won and lost in the markets almost every day, but most people these days utilize the financial markets for the rewards they can offer to *all* of us, not just the very rich. Most people have far less money to invest than those barons you read about.

Most people in fact, are normal people with normal jobs, normal incomes and average assets.

Your forty thousand dollars that you don't know quite what to do with, will get you the services of most any broker available today. Twenty thousand dollars will certainly get you in the door. In fact, while there may still be some stock brokers who have minimum numbers that they work with, most stock brokers today will work with almost anyone. You can't call up a broker trying to turn two thousand or even ten thousand dollars into fifty or sixty thousand in the next five business days. But if you are a realistic investor with realistic goals for the two thousand dollars that you can set aside, most brokers will listen to you, and they will offer you suggestions. Your two thousand dollars won't do much for you if you're interested in purchasing individual stocks, but you can easily buy into a mutual fund. Some mutual funds have returned better than fifty percent in a good year and average fifteen to twenty percent. Match that against the two to six percent return of your CD or money market.

Your broker won't make much money for himself helping you with your two thousand. In some firms, he may not even make anything. But you have to understand something here. The brokerage business is a business of building relationships. It's a people business. One *on* one and one *by* one. If you walk in to a broker's office with your two thousand dollars and he doesn't treat you as well as he can, are you going to return to him when you inherit two hundred big ones, or perhaps win the lottery? Are you going to refer your parents or friends to him? Your two thousand dollars deserves respect, and so do you. In most cases, you will get that respect if you call your friendly stock broker. There are still clients that think their five hundred thousand dollars is an intrusion on the broker's time. Most brokers only wish they had a hundred such clients.

You do have to understand one thing with your small account. You are not going to receive the majority of your broker's attention. He is not going to call you every week with an update on how you're doing unless he's a very new broker with not much else to do. You may not hear from him for awhile. You may develop questions that you need answered. The remedy? Call him. Every so often, call your broker to see how things are going. If you have a question, hop on the phone. Your broker may not be able to call *you* every week. His focus is obviously on the larger accounts that feed him. But if he has a problem with you occasionally calling *him*, find another broker. And use the new broker when you score on that lottery!

When you buy these stocks, bonds, stock funds, bond funds, or whatever, you must realize that there are a lot of things going on in the markets. The financial markets are constantly changing. The stock broker's calling in life is to be there to explain these changes to you when they're happening, and to help you adjust your portfolio as these changes develop.

If all of this is beginning to sound too good to be true, there's a reason. It is. There are problems. Your broker deals with many different conflicts.

In order to learn about the environment in which your broker works, and the environment in which he deals, we will be exploring his world in much more detail.

If you now use a broker, or if you should decide you want to, knowing a little more about the environment he operates in, will make you a more savvy investor.

Why do I need a Stock Broker?

2

Why do I need a stock broker?

How many times I've heard this question. It may be in a seminar or simply with a group of people in a social setting. After thinking about the question more than just a little bit, I think I've developed a standard answer. I would like to share it with you now. Why do you need a stock broker?
Maybe you don't!

There are two types of people in the world with money to invest.
Those who know something about money,
and those who don't.
Those who are knowledgeable about money and investing, proceed to invest their funds in order to realize maximum returns consistent with the investment risks they are willing to accept. If they are real knowledgeable investors, they may not require or use the services of a stock broker. Then again they may. They may be quite content and very successful using whatever means that are at their disposal to efficiently put their money to work. Many knowledgeable investors however, also appreciate the "value added" that a financial professional can bring them in their quest to maximize the returns on their money.

Those who know little or nothing about money fall into two additional sub-categories.

Those who know nothing but think they do,
and those who realize they know nothing.

Those who know nothing about money but think they do, will rarely if ever seek the services of a financial professional. If they even recognize themselves while reading this book, they will become immediately insulted and heave these pages into the nearest trash can. They shouldn't. It is not the intent of this book to insult anyone. Our purpose here is to offer ideas and suggestions that will make everyone smarter investors. Besides, I have a special affinity for these people. In my early years—I was one of them! If they refuse to learn however, this group will eventually become very successful at one thing—*losing their money.* Not to worry. The rest of us need these people. In order to make serious money in the financial markets we have to take it from someone else. These people are the "someone elses." After they have managed to turn a hundred thousand dollars into about five thousand, they have been known to wander into brokerage offices seeking the advice of brokers.

"Can you turn this five thousand dollars back into the one hundred thousand it used to be?" Not likely.

The one thing financial professionals really wish this group *would* learn is not to share their wisdom with others. They often know just enough to be dangerous and their ideas can seriously hurt people who innocently take their advice.

Those who have money but realize they know little about it fall into two additional groups.

Those who will never invest,
and those who seek help.

Those who will never invest, will never invest for two reasons. The first reason is that they heard horror stories about the "investor" we just talked about or took his advice and promptly lost money. It scared them, and now they think that every one who invests, loses their money. They will be more than happy to leave their money in short term certificates of deposit or money market funds, allowing the banks or brokerage firms they deal with to reap the excess returns. The banks and brokerages love these people. By simply guaranteeing the investment principal they can re-invest this person's money and profit on the spread. It simply doesn't get any better. If you don't agree, re-examine many of the bank advertisements you see today. They take delight in *re-enforcing* such fears.

"Sleep tight, knowing your money is earning "x" percent and is "safe!" Perhaps, but smart investors usually *lose sleep* thinking about such poor returns!

The second reason people will never invest is quite simple. From whatever the sources, these people already have enough money to live comfortably off of, for the rest of their lives. These individuals really don't care about forgoing the natural return on their money. They simply can't be bothered, nor do they need to be. The banks and money market purveyors of the world *really* love these people—for the same reasons they love the people who are scared. The difference is that these people have a lot more money for them to make their profit off of. To grow their liquid assets and keep up with inflation, these people must have enough excess income even with the lower returns, to consistently add much of it back into their principal.

This then, leaves us with the people who have money, accept the fact that they know little or nothing about it, but are not willing to simply give away the returns that are rightfully theirs.

These people again, fall into two separate groups. (Is this getting boring? I hope not, because it's real life and I'm just about finished.)

The first group simply has no interest in things financial. These people have their own areas of expertise and are more than willing to avail themselves of the financial professional. The second group also acknowledges that they have little knowledge of money but they are more than anxious to learn.

Both of these groups will seek the advice of a financial professional and since the modern day stock broker is one of the finest and most capable financial professionals available today, these people will often end up retaining the services of the broker. In doing so, they will form a relationship that they can build on. Over time the stock broker will continue to educate them until, perhaps they actually need his services less. They will become people who truly have learned—and now really do know, something about money. They may still however, recognize the "value added" of the stock broker in their continuing quest to maximize the returns on their money.

Why do you need a stock broker? You may not. But people who utilize the services of a stock broker are either people who know something about money, they are people who don't anything about money but eventually will, or they are people who really don't know much about money and don't care to. Their common trait is that they refuse to give away the potential returns that their money can earn—returns that are rightfully theirs. These people are willing to pay for financial expertise. They feel it's money very well spent!

What kind of investments are there?

3

What kind of investments are there?

This chapter involves a discussion of the basic concepts of investing. It also explains the differences between various types of investments and investment vehicles. Those of you who already know the difference between stocks, bonds, limited partnerships and the like, may wish to move directly to Chapter III or you may wish to read this chapter as a quick review. Those of you who may be considering the idea of investing for the first time, should consider this chapter a primer on investing.

The entire world of investing can be broken down into two simple concepts. When you invest your money, you either purchase ownership of something, or you loan your money out to someone else.

Taking these simple concepts one step further, you usually purchase ownership in order to grow your money. You want the value of what you purchased to become worth more than you paid for it. The purchase of a valuable work of art or a collectors item is investing. You hope that over time, you will be able to sell your purchase for more than you paid for it—usually considerably more. You also accept the idea that it may become worth less than what you bought it for. With the potential for greater gain, comes the risk of loss.

When you "loan out" your money, you expect payment for the use of that money. This payment is most often called "interest." The payment or interest that you receive for the use of your money is yours to use as you please. You do not expect your investment to grow significantly in value unless you allow the borrower to keep the payments, and use them too, paying you yet more, for use of the additional funds. In either event, you can only expect to get paid the agreed amount of interest, and the full amount of money you loaned out, at an agreed point in time.

Stocks are a purchase of ownership. Companies that divide up their ownership into certificates of ownership (stocks) are called corporations. Some corporations only allow certain people to buy their stock. These are called "private corporations" and you cannot buy ownership in them unless the other owners allow you to. Other corporations are called "public corporations". They allow the public at large to purchase their shares. When you purchase stock certificates in a corporation, you are purchasing part ownership in that corporation. You now own a percentage or "share" of the company. The stock certificates you receive are formal recognition of your ownership and in fact, are often called "shares". You are allowed to vote for who runs the company. The power of your vote depends on how many of the company shares you own. It is fair to say that someone who owns a large percentage of the company will have far more say about how it is run, than someone who owns a very small share. Regardless, you will be asked for your vote, in what is called a "proxy". The company will actually send you forms that you can fill out. You can cast your vote on various matters, and you can mail the form back to them. Your votes will be formally entered into the records of the company. Together with all of the other votes received, you will direct how the company is run by its management. Not incidentally, the company's management works for you and the other shareholders. You are the "owners" of the company.

There are three types of value associated with your shares of stock. The first is called "par value." It is usually a very small dollar amount and for our purposes here, par value means absolutely nothing. It is an accounting technique for record keeping purposes only. The only reason you need to know about par value is that it appears on the certificates you get. If you just paid $59.00 for a share of stock and receive back a certificate that clearly states "Par Value $1.00" you want to know that you didn't just lose $58.00. The second value of our shares is called "book value." In the calculation of book value, the entire value of the corporation is divided up by the number of shares issued and the result is the book value for each individual share. This too, is an irrelevant number for our purposes although it does give you information that is useful. If the corporation was liquidated and every little piece of it was sold separately, every desk, every computer, all the land, all of the inventory; then this book value per share, is approximately what you could expect to receive back as partial owner of the company.

The *real* value of your shares is the "market value." This is the value assigned to your shares by all of the people who are willing to buy them, or are thinking of selling them in a free market. This is the value you see quoted in the stock listings each night. This is the value you pay or receive for your stock. Many factors go into establishing the market value. How much money is available to buy the stock? Are there better values to be had? How quickly is the company growing? What did they earn during the last quarter or year? What are they going to earn next year? What is the business climate in the industry in which they do business? What is the current economic climate?

If you were to buy a local stationary store, you would

probably be doing it for two reasons. First you would want to pay yourself a salary. Second, you would want to build the store into a larger, more profitable operation so that, when you sold it, you would get more (hopefully much more) than what you paid for it. If you didn't think the store could make you more money than you could earn by simply loaning the money out, you wouldn't buy the store. You would loan the money out and save yourself a whole lot of aggravation. When you buy stock, you operate on the same principle. You want to make more money on the stock than you could by simply loaning it out. That's why people buy stocks. Buying stocks is called "growth investing." You want your money to "grow."

When you loan out your money, it is called "income investing".

If you buy a bond, note or perhaps a treasury bill, you have loaned out your money. A certificate of deposit? Same thing. If you keep money in a money market account you are loaning it out. For a very short period of time perhaps, but it's still a loan.

Short period of time? What does that mean? The "term" of your loan means everything. It is the amount of time you agree to loan out your money for.

All things being equal (and they never are) the longer you have until your borrower has to pay you back, the more interest you should get paid. You are taking a greater risk that your borrower could run into financial trouble and not be able to pay you. When you invest in a certificate of deposit you know the exact term of the loan. You have a maturity date. A money market? You can get it back any time you want it, thus the lower rate.

Longer term loans in the investment world usually come in the form of "bonds." When you buy a bond, the original term of the loan is usually for a number of years. It could range from three to as many as thirty years. A bond usually pays more interest than the short term loan. If you loan your money to your brother-in-law or another individual it isn't usually very liquid. You usually can't sell that kind of loan if you decide you need your money back. When you buy bonds, you can. As formal (and legally binding) evidence of your loan, you are issued a certificate—and the certificate is "negotiable." You can sell it to someone else at any time for whatever they will pay you for it. This is where most people lose money on bonds. It's the "whatever they will pay you for it" part!

Over the term of the loan, the bond's actual value will fluctuate. In any economy, the demand for money is constantly changing. When demand is strong, borrowers are willing to pay more for the use of your money. Interest rates rise. When the demand for your money is not so great, the borrowers are willing to pay less and interest rates fall. If you originally purchase a bond when interest rates are 10%, your borrower agrees to pay you 10%, period. That income stream does not change over the course of your loan. It was agreed to. But the demand for money changes. Lets say four years into your loan, the demand for money drops and current loans can be had for 8%. Your bond is still paying 10% on the original amount you loaned out (bought the bond for). If you decide you need your money back, you are not going to sell that bond at what you paid for it. You are going to raise the price to a point where the new buyer, based on the new price, only gets the *current rate* of 8%, on your bond. If you don't raise the price yourself, you don't have to worry about it. The financial markets will do it for you. The financial markets know what your bond is worth. Conversely, if the current interest rates increase, the value of your bond will decrease. Your 10% bond is going to be worth less in a 12% market. In short, when you buy a long term bond, its value to someone else will rise or fall opposite the rise or fall of current interest rates. This is called "interest rate volatility". You don't have to worry about this if you are able to hold your bond until it matures. You know then, that you will get your original value back, no matter what the interest rate is. It's when you need the money back *before the bond matures* that problems develop. You may have to take much less (or may actually receive much more) than what you originally paid for the bond.

Why would anyone buy bonds, then, if the risk of losing money is so great? If you can go out and buy a certificate of deposit from a bank and know that in two years you get your money back, why take the risk with the bonds?

Two reasons. First, you can usually (not always) get more income from the longer term bond. Remember. You are taking more risk of default, and for that reason, you are receiving more interest on the bond. The second and far more important reason, is to lock in the higher interest rate for a *longer period of time*.

There is risk in *either* of these two investments. You just have to understand what the different risks are, that's all. If you need income to live off of, and you buy a short term certificate while interest rates are high, you don't risk the principal (the original amount) that you loaned out. You risk the *continued income* from it. When the two year certificate that you bought at 8% comes due, and current interest rates have dropped to 2%, you now have to loan your money back out at the lower rate. Your income just dropped by 75% and if you were using that income to buy groceries and gifts for the grandchildren during the holidays, that "pay cut" really hurts.

In short, if you want to protect your *principal* (the money you loan out), you buy the short term certificates and take whatever interest they give you. If, on the other hand, you prefer to protect your *income*, you "lock it in" with the longer term bonds. Once you agree to the rate on the longer term bond, your income doesn't change for as long as you own it.

There are a couple of additional things you should consider when investing for income. You can loan your money out to many different people or entities and you can buy bonds from just about all of them. You can loan your money to the U.S. Government in the form of treasury bonds. You can loan it to corporations. Corporations issue stock but they also borrow money. These are called corporate bonds. You can loan it out to individuals. Most home mortgages are packaged (placed together in pools) and sold as bonds. Of course no discussion of bonds would be complete without a mention of "tax free" bonds. When you loan your money to individual states or any of their local municipalities, the income they pay you is not taxable by the federal government, thus the term "tax free." If you loan money to the state you live in, or one of its municipalities, your state usually doesn't tax the income either, thus the term "double tax free." Cities within the state can't tax you either, thus the firm "triple tax free."

Unless you own tax free bonds you can't possibly appreciate how much fun it is to fill out your tax return. All of that tax free income is placed on line 8b, of your 1040 return. No taxes on that income! Regardless, you should understand that when you buy a tax free bond it is just that, a "bond", with all of the characteristics of any other type of bond.

When you loan your money out, it is also wise to consider whether the borrower has enough financial strength to pay you back both your interest and principal. Some borrowers buy insurance for their bonds. Insured bonds almost always carry the highest credit rating. Thus the term "insured bonds." Some borrowers are ready to go bankrupt or perhaps are just starting up their business and have very poor credit ratings. They are very high risk borrowers and must pay much more interest to borrow money. Their bonds are commonly known as "high yield bonds" or by their more familiar name, "junk bonds".

You now understand the two basic investment concepts. You buy stocks for growth and you loan your money out in order to receive income. But there are many more investments available. The investments we are now going to discuss don't really stray from the two concepts we have been talking about. It's just that these investments are so common they can easily be construed as "different." They fall into two categories. They are either *derivatives* of growth and income investing, or they are *different methods* of investing in growth or income. Lets look a couple of popular derivatives first.

Limited partnerships and Real Estate Investment Trusts are two investment opportunities available. One could challenge whether they are derivatives in the strictest sense of the term but their objectives are still that of growth, income or both so I will take the liberty of placing them in this part of the book.

Limited partnerships are specialized investments. If you decided you wanted to buy a two family house, fix it up, rent it for five or ten years and then sell it for a profit, you might not have enough money to do it. You could take on a partner in your endeavour. Limited partnerships are a more formal and complex way of doing just that. If you buy into a limited partnership you are a partner, not a corporate shareholder. If you want out of the partnership you have to find another partner to take your place. This might not be so easy, especially if your little venture hasn't worked out as well as you hoped it would. Most limited partnerships do not trade openly in the markets, as do stocks. Some trade like stocks, but far more of them trade only between the partners and potential partners. While many limited partnerships offer very good investment potential, many haven't worked out so well. If a partnership doesn't trade openly and you want to get out of it, you are going to have considerable trouble selling your interest. You may not get anything near what it is actually worth because the new buyer may not want to pay what it is worth. The concern here is "liquidity." If there isn't an established and on-going price for your interest in the partnership, there are no guarantees that you can sell it when you want to, and no guarantees that anyone else will want to buy it at its fair value. Limited partnerships are usually investments in real estate, oil drilling or other very high potential endeavours.

Real Estate Investment Trusts, or REITS have become very popular recently. One could think of these as mutual funds that invest in real estate rather than stocks or bonds. Most are listed on either the American or New York stock exchanges insuring their liquidity. If you want to purchase a real estate venture, this is a quick and easy way to do it. Like stocks, however, they take on a value of their own which can be more or less than the value of the actual ventures they own. Most are structured to both grow in value, and pay dividends. Think of REITS as both a growth and income investment.

Options are definitely derivatives. When you buy an option on a stock you are not buying the stock. You are not buying the ownership. Instead, you are contracting with someone else to either buy or sell the stock at a specified price during a specified period of time. You could for example buy a contract from someone in which you both agree that the other person will sell you 100 shares of a certain stock for a certain price during the next two months. Such a contract is called a "call" on the stock. You may think the price of a certain stock currently at $50.00, will rise to $70.00 in the two months. Someone who currently owns the $50.00 stock may be very happy to accept $52.00 for it. He agrees to sell you his stock for $50.00 anytime during the next two months and he charges you $2.00 for the agreement. If the stock increases during the next two months, you can exercise your option and buy his stock at $50.00. You can then turn around and sell it at what ever increased price it is worth. The advantage is called "leverage." Leverage is when you get far more use from your money than you normally would—and far more risk. In this case, you controlled the ownership of a $50.00 stock for two months. Instead of buying it for the $50.00 it cost you only $2.00. If the stock went up to $60.00, you made $8.00 on a $2.00 investment (the $10.00 increase less the $2.00 you paid for the option). That's a gain of 400% (the $8.00 gain divided by the $2.00 investment). If you had bought the stock at $50.00 the $10.00 gain in price would have only been 20% (the $10.00 gain divided by $50.00). Of course if the stock remained at the same price or went down, you lost your entire investment. In reality, you don't actually have to buy or sell the stock. The options take on their own values, based on the price movement of the underlying stock. You simply buy and/or sell the options.

Options sound easy. They sound like, and are fun. It's amazing how much money you can lose playing the option game. There are very conservative strategies and very risky ones. Don't play this game unless you really know what you are doing or have a broker who really knows his "options".

You now know you can invest in income or growth but

there are many ways to go about doing either—many different "vehicles" you can use. Some of these vehicles are so popular that they are almost considered investments all by themselves. The important thing to understand, however, is that these "vehicle investments" maintain the same characteristics as the fundamental investments that they actually consist of.

In a mutual fund you pool your money with many other investors in order to buy stocks, bonds or both. You also pay the "fund manager" to invest the funds. Sometimes the fund managers do a real good job and sometimes they don't. In a mutual fund you also reap the benefits of "diversification." Your money is able to buy many different stocks or bonds as opposed to the few you would be able to buy independently with the same amount of money. If a single investment should happen not to work out, it is a small part of the whole portfolio. Your risk of loss is reduced.

There are many different types of mutual funds but they can be simplified. When you first look at a fund you want to know what it invests in. If you are looking for growth, you don't want to buy a fund that invests in only tax free bonds. Mutual funds are available these days for just about any type of investment you may desire, and they are managed by both successful and unsuccessful managers. If you purchase a fund that invests only in a single state's tax free long term bonds you can expect that fund to perform much like the bonds themselves do. The value of its shares will go up and down inversely to current interest rates and the income it pays will be triple tax free if you live in that state.

The second thing you want to know about your fund is its structure. There are two basic structures for mutual funds. Open end and closed.

When you purchase shares of an open end fund, you add to the fund's available capital. When you sell shares, the fund has to pay you out of its assets. The funds total value therefore, constantly rises or falls based not only on the rise and fall of its individual investments, but also because money is constantly flowing in and out of the fund. Regardless of how much money is currently in the fund, its net asset value is derived from dividing the total value of the holdings by the number of current shares outstanding. In the case of the open end fund, this is the only value that counts. You will always sell at the net asset value. You will always buy at the net asset value plus whatever commission the fund charges, if any. The net asset value is quoted daily so you know exactly how much it is worth, and how much you can sell it for.

Oops! Did we just use a dirty word? "Commission"? None of us (including brokers) like paying commissions but there's a problem here. Mutual funds are big business and like any big business they must advertise what they have to offer. Commissions are one way of doing that. Expenses are another. All funds pay their managers through expenses charged to the fund, but they can advertise in different ways. One way is to charge a commission, which is partially paid to your broker who not only explained the fund to you, but also explained why it was the *right one* for you. Another way is not to use the services of a broker. The fund advertises on television and in magazines instead. Six hundred thousand dollars for thirty seconds has to come from somewhere. What do these funds do? They pay these bills out of "expenses" instead of "commission charges."

You may choose to pay no commission at all. Funds that charge no commission are called "no load" funds. You are on your own now, since there is no broker to help you decide which fund to buy. You must look to advertising, newsletters, a prospectus (a pamphlet that is the legal explanation of the fund) or other means to determine what the fund invests in, how good it is, and whether or not you should continue to keep your money invested in it. Since most no load funds advertise heavily in the media it stands to reason that the media are very courteous to those advertising dollars, when they write up an analysis of the fund. No load funds usually have much higher expenses than the commission funds, in order to pay for their advertising. Since the expenses come from the profits of the fund, if you buy this fund, you are in effect, paying forever.

You may choose to pay the commission up front, get the advice of a knowledgeable broker, and not have to worry about all of those additional advertising expenses that go on forever. If you do this, you are paying what is known as a "front end load."

You may choose to buy a commission fund, get the advice, but not pay the commission when you buy it. You decide you will only pay commission if you sell it before a certain time expires. The time varies with the fund. Your broker will still receive his commission for his advice. How do you arrange this deal? You buy what is called a "back end load". This fee arraignment is sort of a compromise. You don't pay any commission when you buy the fund, but you do pay if you sell it before a certain amount of time, and you still pay more expenses over the life of the fund. Some would consider you "trapped!" The fund still has to pay your broker, but if paying a commission bothers you, this is an option. You always get what you pay for.

It really doesn't matter which way you decide to pay— as long as you understand *how* you're paying, and *what you're getting for it*. Let's make the decision a little easier by suggesting an analogy.

You decide you need to drive a new car.

Do you buy the car for cash? Then you buy the front load fund. You pay up front and you own it.

Do you buy the car on time, taking out a loan? Then

you buy the equivalent back end load fund.

Do you want to lease the car? Then buy the no load fund!

In a "closed end" fund, the manager raises a certain amount of money and then "closes" the fund. No more money comes in or goes out of the fund. The shares are then listed on a stock exchange where you can buy and sell them any time you want. Unlike the open end fund, the closed end fund manager knows exactly how much money he has to invest. He can more precisely take positions in his investments of choice. He isn't forced to buy or sell investments because of the constant flow of money in and out of his portfolio. Like the open end funds, the "net asset value" is determined daily by dividing the value of the assets held, by the number of shares outstanding. In the open end funds, however, this value may not always be what you pay or receive on the shares when you decide to buy or sell them. Just as that corporation stock does, the shares of the open end fund take on a market value which may be greater or less than the actual value of the holdings. Why? Investors may be willing to pay more than the actual value of the holdings because it's easier to buy the fund than go out and buy the individual holdings. Perhaps the fund invests in foreign stocks that are not even available to individual investors. Perhaps the performance of the fund is poor. Investors may not even be willing to pay as much as the holdings are worth, because they feel they can get better performance elsewhere.

When a closed end fund sells for more than its net asset value, it is said to be selling for a "premium." If it sells for less, it's selling at a "discount." A lot of very smart people like to buy discounted funds. Where else can you purchase investments for less that they are actually worth? Before you buy the discounted fund though, you may want to ask yourself why a lot of other very smart people *don't* want to own it. You can be sure your broker is asking himself that question.

The final investment vehicle we want to discuss in the annuity. There are basically two types, the fixed and the variable. The fixed annuity invests in fixed income securities, an income investment. The variable annuity is much more interesting. It usually consists of a number of different mutual funds that can range from money market funds to various stock and bond funds. In a variable annuity you can constantly switch part or all of your money from one of its funds to another. The variable annuity can be either income, growth or both, depending on the mutual funds it offers, and those you or your broker select.

The annuity simply takes the investing concept and ties it up in a nice little insurance package. Why would you want to do that? Because annuities are tax deferred, that's why. Another not too incidental feature, is that many annuities insure the amount of your original investment, in the event you should die. Where else could you buy stocks and know that in the event of a downturn in the market, and if you die, your heirs will receive at least the original amount of your investment?

Annuities may be presented to you as a very simple way to invest money. On the surface they are, but you may want to read the fine print. While the general concepts are straight forward, the varied terms of different annuities can be mind boggling. For this reason many of the people who sell them don't know all of the consequences, and you won't either until you decide you want *out*.

In an annuity, the taxes that you would otherwise pay to your favorite uncle (Sam) are instead re-invested—to earn income, or to grow along with the investment you originally made. Over a number of years the difference in final return (because you were able to re-invest those "would have been taxed dollars") can be substantial. Annuities come with some "hooks" though.

The first hook is the withdrawal of your funds. If you put money into an annuity and then decide to take it all out before you reach age 59 1/2, the government penalizes you by taxing the entire amount withdrawn, at 10%. Put simply, you get only 90% of your money. In addition, you pay your normal income tax rate, on the money that was earned. With very rare exception, you don't want to purchase an annuity if you are going to need the money back before you turn 59 1/2 years old.

The second hook is the surrender charge. You don't pay any commission to buy an annuity but if you want to get out, the surrender charge (commission) works much like the back end load fund we talked about. Only it's often much more onerous.

Annuities don't charge you a commission when you buy them, but they definitely pay the person who sold them to you. When you buy an annuity you are usually paying your salesman, banker or broker between three and five percent of the entire amount of money you invest. Where do annuities get the money to pay those commissions? Out of the returns of the annuity, of course! The performance of an annuity will almost always be less than the performance of its underlying investment for that very reason.

This is how your annuity salesman looks at annuities. You can invest your money in certificates of deposits, in which case he gets paid nothing. Or you can invest it in an annuity in which case he gets paid plenty. The money you earn on the certificate of deposit is taxable to you. With the annuity you only pay taxes when you take your earnings out of the annuity, but of course, the annuities usually earn you less. In most instances, the net after tax result is about the same.

When your certificate of deposit comes due, you "roll it over" and your salesman again, gets paid nothing. When your annuity comes due, your salesman will definitely find you a better rate with *another* insurance company. Why? So he can get paid again.

Meanwhile, you suffer all of the restrictions of being in the annuity. Surrender charges, withdrawal penalties and the like. In short, if you take your CD money and buy an annuity, your annuity salesman has "trapped you." He gets paid on your money when he otherwise wouldn't have. Since you have to pay the taxes when you *take your money out* of the annuity, *you probably won't.* Thus the salesman keeps getting paid every time your annuity matures.

You should buy an annuity as part of a comprehensive tax deferral strategy. You shouldn't buy it because there is "no commission" and you think you're getting something for nothing. Used correctly, an annuity can be a superb investment. If used incorrectly, it's a great way for annuity salespeople to elicit commissions from those who want financial advice, but don't want to pay for it. If used incorrectly, an annuity can provide you with a substantial financial nightmare—but you get what you pay for.

Countless volumes of information have been written on the many different types of investing. This overview is not meant to be a detailed one but it should allow new investors a basic understanding, as we continue to pursue your stock broker's world.

How does the
stock brokerage
business work?

4

How does the stock brokerage business work?

Stock brokers come from all walks of life. Rarely does one start a career as a stock broker fresh out of college. Seldom will you deal with a stock broker who has had no other career experiences than that of the brokerage industry. Teachers, salespeople, people who got fed up with corporate management and dropped out of big business, ex-military officers—all are in the brokerage company ranks.

One of the most successful brokers I ever met came from chemical sales. A true "cold call cowboy" (one who spends countless hours on the telephone prospecting day and night), he built his business rapidly, rarely stopping to notice that he knew very little about investing. It didn't matter to him and it didn't matter to his office. He was a likable guy. His office manager and fellow brokers helped him. He would learn the details of investing as time went on.

New clients and new money are everything in the brokerage business and, if someone is willing to spend seventy or more hours on the telephone soliciting people, that money *will* come.

A stock broker must be licensed. Even to recommend investments to you over the telephone, the broker must have a license. The next time you receive an unsolicited call asking you to invest in something, ask for the person's name and ask if he has a license. If he is simply inviting you to a seminar and is not recommending an investment, he doesn't need to be licensed but if he starts to recommend or explain investments to you and doesn't have a license, hang up and don't believe a word of what he said. Without the license he simply doesn't know what he is talking about.

What kind of license should stock brokers have? Every retail broker you work with should have a series 7 securities license. Most will also have an insurance license, allowing them to sell annuities. A series 6 license allows them to sell only a limited repertoire of investment selections, primarily mutual funds. The series 7 covers it all: stocks, bonds, mutual funds, limited partnerships and options. The insurance license wraps it up because a broker can only sell fixed annuities or life insurance if he has an insurance license. In order to sell variable annuities (the ones which offer a selection of stock funds within the annuity umbrella) your broker must have both the insurance license *and* a series 7. There are lots of advisors out there, but if yours (or the one you are interviewing) doesn't have at least a series 7, don't deal with him. His selection of alternatives is far too limited. Because of those limitations you can be sure that the few ideas he *is* able to offer you will always be presented as your best possible alternatives. They have to be. They're his *only* alternatives! If your broker has the insurance license and the series 7, he has a broad selection of investments to choose from. This broader selection will allow him to truly choose what's best for you. If you really like the person and he doesn't have an insurance license, you can live with it. Buy your investments from him, and your insurance from an insurance agent.

Just keep in mind that there may be times when an insurance situation would be the right idea for you. If your broker isn't licensed to sell it, or is unfamiliar with insurance concepts, you may not be getting the most unbiased advice.

The series 7 is not an easy examination. There are lawyers, MBA's, teachers and other very educated people who have had to take it two or three times in order to pass it. Most brokers in the business for over two years would probably fail it if they had to take it again without studying. There is much information that must be memorized for the series 7 test. Once in the business, however, a broker forgets much of the knowledge because it just isn't needed very often.

If your broker passes the series 7, he has the mechanics and he has the law. He still doesn't have the experience. He still doesn't have the reality of the business. It's nice for him to understand the mechanics of a given mutual fund before he presents it to a first time buyer, but it's much nicer for him to understand the reality of the situation. He isn't going to understand the reality of recommending what people should do with their money until he has a few years of experience under his belt.

Let's say you are a retired couple who goes to see a broker. He recommends an investment, and you put all of your years of hard earned dollars into it; you can't go back and earn it again. If, two days after you invested, the recommendation has lost you ten percent of your money, that's *reality*. When you call your broker back to discuss it, you are going to give him a serious "reality check." It's a sobering experience for the broker. If he's had that experience a few times it makes him think just a little longer about you and the investment he's recommending to you.

A broker may understand all about how an investment

works, but being able to choose the right investment for someone else comes only from years of experience.

As with any business, the investment brokerage business is all about making money—money for the client, the broker and for his company.

You make money if the investments your broker places you in, make money. But how does your broker get paid? How does his company make money?

The business of a stock broker can be very lucrative or it can be just okay. One thing the business does not provide, is a steady paycheck. It's a commission business. Your broker may suggest to you that he gets paid a salary, but be assured he would starve if he had to live off the salary they pay him. Every week, every month and every year, your broker starts off with only an inkling of what the future holds for him in terms of income.

With this uncertainty, however, comes potential, and the ability to set his own pace. As with any commission business, your stock broker doesn't settle for guaranteed anything. With the risk of a bad month or year comes the potential for a great one. Any broker still in the business after a few years is probably making a decent living, but it's the potential that continues to drive him.

People have some very unrealistic ideas of just what a broker's earnings are. Most people think that the stock broker is making far more than he may be. His is a very tough business. If your broker was really wealthy, he could retire and live off of his own investments.

Your broker's income is all about production and payout. What your broker acquires in gross commissions is called his "production." That commission amount you see on your confirmation slips when you buy or sell, is his production. Depending on his capabilities, experience, and operational method, your broker can produce upwards of $200,000 a year. A beginner might produce far less and a super star could be running his business at a million or more. Lets place the average experienced broker at somewhere between $200,000 to $250,000 of production in a decent year.

"Wow!" you say. "Not bad. Those guys really do take in some money."

Wait a minute. That's his production. That's not what *he* gets paid. The interesting part to your broker, is his "payout." Your broker only gets to keep a percentage of that production figure, and the percentage he keeps is called his payout.

Depending on who your broker works for, his payout can vary. It commonly varies from thirty percent to around forty five. The largest companies often pay out the least amounts with the smaller ones usually paying more. Payout can be the same regardless of the type of investment, or it can vary with different investment types. In a variable payout system, stocks might pay out 40% while insurance pays out 50%.

Some firms also offer a higher payout for their own products. If your broker is recommending a mutual fund that is run by his company, you may want to know if he's getting a higher payout on it as opposed to a mutual fund run by another company. Ask him.

There is another common scheme that many brokerage companies use in order to encourage their brokers to work a bit harder. This type of system is known in the industry as "grid payout." How does the grid work? Like this. The more the broker produces, the higher the payout percentage for *all* of that production. Lets put it all together and see what it means.

Lets assume your broker is an average producer cranking out $250,000 in production for the year. If he's on a thirty percent payout, the firm he works for pays him

$75,000 per year for his trouble and keeps the rest. If he does $200,000 in production, he's working for $60,000 a year.

If he quits his company and goes to a firm that gives him forty percent for his efforts, our $200,000 producer just went from a take home pay of $60,000 to take home of $80,000 per year. The two-fifty guy went to a "buck" ($100,000) from $75,000. Payout means *a lot* to your broker.

A broker who is not on the grid gets the same payout regardless of what his annual production is but a grid producer has a different set of problems.

The grid production system rewards higher production, and often *punishes* length of service (experience) at the same time. It works something like this. A broker with one to five years of experience might receive a thirty percent payout on production of up to $199,999.99. When his production reaches exactly $200,000 (not a penny less) he reaches his first grid level and his payout is increased to thirty *two* percent—retroactively to his first dollar of production during the year. He immediately receives that extra two percent payout on all of the production he has already done, or in this case, a check for $4,000. It's a nice night out. For the rest of the year, he receives the new payout of thirty two percent. His following year's payout begins at the new thirty two percent number. If he doesn't make his grid in the coming year, the company *takes away* the extra two percent that they already paid him. That's right. They *deduct* it from his paycheck at the end of the year. Happy holidays!

That's our one to five year broker. When the broker starts year six with the company, the grid target increases. Now he has to do $250,000 in production to receive the extra two percent payout. At year seven his grid goes to perhaps $275,000. It goes on and on. Your grid broker has a definite incentive to increase his production with each year he's in the business.

What exactly does it take to do $200,000 in annual commissions? Your broker has to invest some serious money. He either has to invest new dollars from new clients, or he has to re-invest the assets of his current clients. How much does he have to invest? At an average commission of 2.5%, in order for our broker to produce $200,000, eight million dollars of client money has to be invested or reinvested each year. (That's $200,000 divided by 2.5%). Is that beginning to look like serious money? To do $250,000, your broker is investing about ten million. To produce one million dollars? You can do the math.

What does it mean to you as his client?

It's now December 15th and the broker's year ends on the 24th. (It's important to note that your broker's years and months, don't end on the last day of the month. Have you ever been called on the third Friday of the month with a great investment idea?) Your happy broker has now done a total of $240,000 in production this year and he has to do $250,000 to make or stay on his grid. To make matters more interesting, that office the company gives him to work in, is up for grabs. The highest producers get the offices. There are a couple of "cold call cowboys" (high volume telephone solicitors) out on the floor with no office, and those long hours of telephone prospecting have added up. Your broker's production is running neck and neck with two of them who are definitely interested in his office. That floor, where all the lower producers sit together, is a fun place to work, but make no mistake about it the office is nicer. Besides, the office makes his clients think that he's important. What would you think if *your* broker lost his office? Are you still going to trust him with your money? Are you going to think he did something wrong?

Your broker is doing some fast calculations.

"$10,000 to make grid and maybe another $5,000 to stay out in front of the cowboys. Ten days to do it in. Hmm. $15,000 divided by average commission of about 2 1/2% equals $600,000. I have to either invest or reinvest $600,000 in the next ten days. The clock's running. At stake? My office, the $5,000 retroactive to the beginning of the year, in pocket and oh yes. The difference in next years payout which could be at least another $5,000."

Oops. He almost forgot. He's not going to get any favors from the sales manager either, because he didn't do very well in the last sales contest. That's right. The one where they wanted him to put $500,000 into the company's latest mutual fund. All he had to do was to put $500,000 of his client's money into the fund and he would have won a Parker Pen.

That wasn't the inspiration though. If he didn't do it, the company decided he wasn't much of a team player anymore. They didn't like him for awhile.

Your experienced broker didn't like anything about the fund. So he didn't put any of his client's money in it. Now is *not* the time for him to be asking the sales manager for any favors, like letting him keep his office. Talk about pressure!

Do you want to be this broker's client during the last ten days of his year? He'll have some investment ideas for you, whether you need them or not.

Of course, if you really like the guy and he's done well by you, and you just happen to have an extra $50,000 laying around that you were thinking about investing, you could make a friend for life.

What does all of this mean to you, the client?

You don't want your broker to be on the grid. If your

broker receives the same payout regardless of his production, he is under far less pressure to move your investments around, just to make his company's numbers. If he is on a grid and you really like him, fine. Just try to understand the pressures he's under. How can you tell if your broker is on a grid? Ask him. A "yes" or a very vague, stumbling answer means he is. If he's not on a grid he should be *more than happy* to tell you. If he doesn't know what you're talking about, he has never been on a grid. He probably doesn't even know how much better off he and his clients are.

You don't want your broker deciding what the best investment for you is, when there's a sales contest going on. His determination as to what is the best investment for *you*, should not be made on the basis of whether or not he wins his pen. His status in the office should not determine what you invest in. How can you tell if there's a sales contest going on? Ask him. He might not give you the right answer, but look for his reaction. You could also tell him you really like the idea but you'll be more interested in three weeks, when your certificate of deposit comes due. All sales contests have deadlines. If he still likes the idea for you after waiting three weeks (and after the deadline has passed), he likes it for what it is, not because he had to make a showing in his company's contest.

You do want your broker to be fairly and consistently compensated for his efforts. Fairness to him, is fairness to you, the client.

If you drop in on your broker and discover that he's lost his office, keep that broker forever. It simply means he doesn't let some of these little details get in the way of what's best for his clients.

Who is your Broker?

5

Who is your Broker?

Rarely do brokers begin and end their careers in the brokerage business. It's just too tough.

If they start at a young age, they eventually burn out. They quit and go find something else to do for a living. If the broker comes into the business later in life he hopes he can keep his sanity until he retires.

There's another reason most young people don't begin their careers in the business. The big houses just don't want them. The brokerage companies can't have someone with such obviously limited experience representing them, even if some clients wouldn't care.

The big shops want experience. The desired experience may vary, but the good brokerage company wants to see broker trainees with some degree of "life experience."

They don't want a person with no life experience representing them and you don't either. That person is not going to be able to empathize with a new retiree that has worked all of his or her life, raised a family, saved a few dollars for retirement, and is now forced to live off of those hard earned dollars.

A widow still grieving from the recent loss of a lifelong partner cannot possible rely on someone so young, to guide her through the investment world. It's not that the young person is not smart. It's not about a lack of sympathy. It's simply that the young person cannot possibly appreciate those circumstances.

Being a broker is all about empathy. Your broker may not be at all like you. His or her circumstances may be quite different than yours. But if your broker can't empathize with you, find another broker.

What was your broker's background? Was it sales? Finance? Corporate? Law? Or was it the host of other backgrounds that make up the highly diverse backgrounds of modern day brokers?

In the early nineteen hundreds, your broker came from wealth. If he didn't he wasn't a broker. The companies loved to hire the sons of wealthy people. What better way to bring in serious dollars than to have someone that was at ease calling all of his rich Daddy's friends for their money? The broker didn't have to be too bright. The firm would tell him where to invest the bucks. All he had to do was get them.

No more. These days, a whole lot of money comes from a whole lot of regular people, and they need brokers who are regular people to relate to them.

Your broker should have a background that you can feel comfortable with. Your broker doesn't have to be from the same occupational background as you, but you should feel comfortable talking to him. You should be able to build a reasonably close relationship.

Obviously, the further removed from the investment business your broker was in his former life, the more years of investment experience you want him to have now.

What is important, is your confidence in this person's ability to handle your money. As a new client, you really don't know enough about this person to have confidence in anyone, so look for the signals. If you've worked hard all your life to scrape out a living, you probably don't want someone whose major concern is making the payments on his leased Porsche. You might prefer someone who has a wife, four kids, two puppy dogs, and a mortgage to feed. That person has to scratch his head every so often to figure out how to pay the bills, just like you do. You can relate. Chat with your broker for a few minutes. Find out what kind of person he is.

All brokers have at least five years of experience in the industry. They have to. They wouldn't do any business if they didn't. Would you take all of your years of retirement money and invest your trust in a broker that came out of the food distribution business and just spent three months getting his brand new broker's license? I wouldn't. So what's a new broker to do? It's simple. They lie.

If you trot into a brokerage house and ask to see a broker, you won't know if he has ten years of experience or ten days. You want a reasonably experienced broker. So how can you tell? If you're an experienced investor, you probably already know. There's a certain knowledge, a certain seasoning that presents itself fairly early on in the conversation. You will determine pretty quickly, how much experience the broker you are talking to, has. If you're a novice it gets trickier, because you really don't know what questions to ask. You have to look for the not so obvious clues. Here are some ideas.

Some novice clients start by asking the broker something about the only stock they know anything about. It may be the twenty shares they got from a company three jobs ago, or a stock that they inherited. If it's a reasonably well known stock the pro will know something about it. Don't be surprised if his knowledge is vague though. There are over five thousand stocks out there, and even the seasoned pro doesn't follow all of them all of the time. Look instead for his reaction.

"I don't follow that one" is a reasonable response but it could be used by a broker with from one day to one decade of experience. What's his reaction? Is it a nervous, frantic search for information on your favorite? Or is it a relaxed straight forward approach? The pro has been asked thousands of times, about stocks he never heard of or perhaps stopped following years ago. His is a calm reaction. "It rings a bell. Was that the one that almost got bought out two years ago?" "Gee, I don't know too much about that company. Lets see what we can find out for you."

Where is your broker sitting? Does he have his own office or is he out on the board room floor? The floor gets the lowest producing brokers. By deduction one could conclude that a new broker is a low producer and thus would be found on the floor. However, you may also have the broker we talked about who lost his office!

You might find a seasoned veteran out there on the floor. You might find a broker that works truly because he loves the business. He doesn't concern himself with the grid or his production. Perhaps he even has other income producing interests. He produces enough commission to keep the house happy, but not to earn the office. He doesn't care. He has enough money of his own. Such a broker might be the find of a lifetime. He has reams of experience, he can guide your investments, and he doesn't worry about how much commission your account generates.

On the other hand that young fellow sitting smugly in the office ten feet away may be a the cold call cowboy. He started digging prospects out of mailing lists a year and a half ago. He interrupted enough people from their dinner time or evening television to eventually find the few who invested their hard earned dollars with him. In fact he found quite a few. Enough to earn him the office. If those calls didn't pay, brokers wouldn't be ringing your telephone off the hook every day.

How old is your broker? If you are talking to a mature broker, it doesn't necessarily mean he has years of experience in the business. He may have changed careers and started in the brokerage business last week. But if he's very young, he obviously doesn't have too many years experience in *any* business. It may seem like common sense but it's easy to become dazzled in that big brokerage office, especially if you are a new investor.

If your broker is really young and you know nothing about the brokerage house you're being asked to invest with, don't. Unscrupulous brokerage companies love the young brokers who can dial for dollars (call people on the telephone for their money) fifteen hours a day. Those young brokers can make lots of money, but it doesn't mean you will.

Here's another sign. By the time any broker has taken the Series 7 examination, he knows a lot of broker jargon. Does this broker speak English to you, or is he trying to impress you with a lot of fancy terms? The seasoned broker may slip once in a while but he realizes that "sixty basis points" means nothing to his client, unless his client happens to trade bonds for a living. He's not going to try to sell you sixty basis points (six tenths of a percent). He's going to suggest it's a little bit over half a percent, or "x" amount of dollars. If you don't understand what the broker is saying, don't buy. Your experienced broker has explained complex terms to first time investors countless times. You will probably understand him.

This brings up another point. Is your broker a teacher? Can he reach out to your level of understanding and explain all of this financial gobbledy gook to you? Fear of the unknown is the worst fear of all. You don't want to be, and cannot afford to be, afraid of investing. But you do need to have at least a basic understanding of what it is you're investing in.

There are basically three types of new investors. Perhaps even seasoned investors fit these categories, but it's not as evident. Which one are you?

The first person wants to know every detail of the investment he or she is purchasing. Person number two only wants to know he can trust his broker. The most common, is the person that wants to get the general idea, and then leaves it up to the broker. This person wants to participate, but realizes full well that he is not an expert.

We will discuss different client types later on but whoever you are, your broker should be able to explain an investment and his reasoning on it, to your reasonable satisfaction.

Keep something in mind though. Investing is an art. You can try to quantify it with charts, company financial statements and all the rest, but the seasoned broker has seen too much. After a while it becomes a feeling. All of the knowledge that he has, melds into a simple "buy", "sell" or "hold." He develops a "sixth sense". If you want your broker to try to sum up his years of experience into a one hour lesson on investing, he won't be able to do it.

There is one final question you should ask yourself about your broker. "Is my money real to him?"

Even a novice broker soon finds himself handling amounts of money that might seem unimaginable to the average person. When dealing with millions of dollars of other people's money not to mention a few dollars of his own, it's easy for the whole thing to become a game. Is your broker treating your hard earned money like so much play money, or does he have a genuine respect for it?

If you're out to find a broker with the latest hot stock for a few thousand dollars of your play money, it may not matter. If, however, you are talking about your serious savings, you want a broker who can respect that. Win lose or draw, all of those wild numbers still come up "green in the 'till".

Who's money is it, anyway?

6

Who's money is it, anyway?

Your broker is judged by his company in many different ways. You may judge him by your own criteria, but his company probably doesn't have the same interests as you do.

Your broker's intelligence, his honesty and his ability to make his clients money, may or may not be of very great concern to his company, depending on the company he works for and the manager of his office. The one thing that does concern them, is your broker's ability to produce commissions. The most important thing that affects your broker's ability to produce commissions, is the size of his "book."

What is the book?

For those of you in other walks of life I would offer a comparison. A broker's book is like your Rolodex. Your contacts greatly affect how you do business. It's all about who you know and such. The broker's book is similar but with a very significant difference. The book has *numbers attached to it*. Specific numbers that change every day with the ups and downs of the markets. The names in your broker's book are his client's names. The numbers in that book are his client's *assets*. Your broker's book consists of all of the clients he has, and the total amount of their assets that he controls. The total amount of money that the broker has under his control, therefore, has come to be known simply as his "book".

Who's money is it? His clients' money of course. But in the brokerage industry there is so much money floating around that the question of who it really belongs to can get kind of fuzzy.

No one single thing counts more to your broker than the size of his book. His peers judge him by it. His management judges him by it. If he ever decides to switch companies, the companies that he interviews will judge him by it. Your broker's book is, in fact, what his business is all about. The size of your broker's book is his image and his power. It is his independence, or his lack of it.

The numbers in those books add up. They are substantial. Your twenty thousand dollars or your eight hundred thousand dollars, combined with the assets of the rest of your broker's clients, add up to millions of dollars. How many millions?

A new broker with a year in the business might have two or three million dollars, or even more under management. An average broker might have a book of ten to thirty million. A seasoned broker with ten or fifteen years in the business could possess a book of fifty million dollars or more. A power broker might run on up to a hundred million dollars—all money under his control, the assets of his clients.

The definition of the "book" comes from the fact that client records are kept on a page in a book. You might be amazed to learn that some of the largest brokerage companies in business today, still rely on that manual page in the book to determine your purchases and sales.

"Oh, I get my statements by computer." you say. Maybe, but unless your statement shows your purchase dates and costs, you are probably still on a manual book.

It takes hours of your broker's time to fill in those pages. The company has billions of dollars of transactions, on little paper pages in a book. Your current holdings are computerized, but the buy and sell records? All on the book. They aren't backed up anywhere and book pages can easily burn in fires. You should know that it is legally the client's responsibility to keep a record of transactions. Don't try to tell the tax people that your broker's records got burned in a fire. They really won't care. If you at least keep the dates of your transactions, your brokerage company may be able to provide micro fiche copies of them for you, usually for a fee. But if you don't keep the dates and your broker's paper book burns, you've got problems.

When you go into a brokers office to open an account, a page is filled out. Your name, address, telephone number, social security number. Income. Net worth. How many children. Job, position. Much of the information the broker asks for may seem unnecessary and quite frankly, a little too personal. You should know, however, that your broker isn't just trying to be nosey when he asks you for all of this information. He is required by law to have it all on file before he does any business with you, whether you like it, he likes it, or not.

Once completed, that page receives an account number and is placed in the "Book" of accounts, a book of clients if you will. Every time you buy or sell, your transaction is supposed to be recorded on the back of the page. Date, price and total dollar. Profit or loss on sale. Some brokers are notorious for keeping an accurate book. Others are equally notorious for ignoring it. Did you ever call your broker at tax time to ask for the original cost basis (purchase price) on an investment you sold during the year? It won't take you more than thirty seconds to figure out which kind of broker you have.

Some conscientious brokers have gotten so disgusted with the archaic system that they have purchased their own computers to record your transactions. Some companies have now done away with the manual book, automatically recording the transactions on computer. It wouldn't hurt for you to ask your broker how he keeps track of your purchases and sales. Remember. You the client, are responsible for those records. It's nice, though if your broker has the numbers instantly available when you're sitting with your tax accountant, and find out that you need that information.

If you should get to thinking that you know more about investing money than your broker, think about all those numbers in his book. When someone is responsible for investing, supervising and monitoring the performance of that kind of money, they have to know quite a bit about it. To put it into perspective there are mutual funds that don't have that kind of money to invest.

As with almost any endeavour in life, one learns from experience. The more experience you have, the more you learn. The more money you have to invest, the more experience you get. Your broker has a lot of money to invest. Unless you are a very experienced investor and you are dealing with a novice as a broker, the broker probably knows more about what is going on in the investment world, than you do.

When you sit down with a broker for the first time to invest your last fifty thousand dollars it might seem like a lot to you. It is, but you must understand that to the broker it's just another fifty or so. Of course the broker should respect you, and the fact that your money is very important to you, but you shouldn't expect him to act as though it's the only fifty thousand that he's ever seen. If he does, make your way quickly to the door with your check book intact, and find another broker!

If your broker recommends investments, and it seems

to you that the recommendation came just a little too fast, or perhaps with not quite enough thought, try to remember this. Your broker probably has very substantial dollars in those same investments or very similar ones.

The broker has watched those investments, perhaps for months or perhaps for years. They may be new ideas to you but they're not new to him. He has seen the investments grow. He's seen them make money for his clients. He has seen them grow in his book. He probably knows the investments better than you do. He has (hopefully) interviewed you and determined what types of investments would be best for you. He has automatically (and maybe very quickly) determined that out of all of the options he could pick from, these are the investments that are right for you. He doesn't manage millions of dollars of client's money and sleep nights, without being pretty good at this sort of thing.

When a good broker comes up with a new investment idea he doesn't just rush out and call every single client in his book. He tries it first, either himself or with some of his more adventurous clients. Then he watches it for a while. When he's totally comfortable with what it can do he begins offering it to the rest of his clients. If he presents a new offering to a lot of his clients, he has reviewed it in detail. He understands the objectives, the potential and the risk. Whether he shares every detail with you probably depends on what kind of client you are, but you can be pretty sure that he knows more about that investment than you may ever know. He has determined to the best of his ability, whether it's good or bad for your account. He has also determined whether it's good or bad for his book. Your broker does not needlessly and wantonly place his book at risk, and you *are* his book.

You should understand another thing when reviewing ideas with your broker. In his business, the customer is *not* always right. In fact the customer is very often—*very* wrong.

It might seem at times, that your broker doesn't treat your money like it's yours. He seems to act like it's "his money". The attitude may seem obnoxious to you at first but think about it for a moment. Would you prefer that he invests your money as if it were merely someone else's money, or as if it were his own? It may be your money, but he thinks of it as his money too. If he *doesn't* think that way, you don't want him to be your broker.

He is always trying to protect you. He wants to keep your money in your account, not someone else's. That "someone else" may be anxiously trying to sell out of what you're dying to buy. He wants to keep you as his client.

The real meaning of the book gets more interesting though. Those assets, turn into commission dollars. This is the book's real importance to your broker and his company.

An average account, in average markets, will generate one to two percent of its total value in commissions.

Lets get specific. You can expect to pay between one and two percent of your account value in commissions. Why? Because of changes (commissioned trades) necessary to keep those assets growing in the ever changing markets. It might be slightly more for an active account and somewhat less for a quiet account that is purely income based, but on the average, your one hundred thousand dollar account can be expected to generate one to two thousand dollars in commission in a given year. The objective obviously, is for your money to achieve greater performance, even after you pay the commissions, than it would have if you had not invested at all.

Lets assume an annual commission rate of one and a half percent is the average.

A broker with a ten million dollar book produces about one hundred fifty thousand dollars in production, the gross commission. At a payout of thirty percent that's forty five thousand for the broker.

The twenty million dollar book doubles it. The thirty million dollar book triples it. Your broker has a book of fifty million? Nice book!

But wait. There's more. That twenty million dollar book that generates ninety thousand to the broker at a thirty percent payout, generates two hundred and ten thousand dollars for his brokerage company.

An average office of say fifteen brokers with average books of fifteen to twenty million apiece? It gets kind of interesting doesn't it?

You can begin to see how brokers and their companies could get into occasional quarrels over who the "books" *really* belong to. Do they belong to the brokers or do they belong to the companies? What does it all mean?

Whoever owns the book claims the right as to what types of investments are recommended for it. If your brokerage company claims ownership of the book, then they also claim that right. They may allow your broker varying degrees of discretion but they have the final word as to what investments you are presented with.

Most brokerage companies have conflicts of interest. They may make a lot of money on the commissions your broker generates but they make a lot more money in many other ways. They run their own mutual funds, for example, and those mutual funds pay them expense fees. They underwrite large offerings of stocks and bonds. When a company wants to offer a new stock or bond they hire an investment banker (often your brokerage company). The investment bankers get paid big commissions to sell these offerings to retail clients. If a company is paying your brokerage company big money to sell their new stock or bond, it doesn't necessarily mean that the investment is a good one. It does mean your brokerage company wants to sell it. It usually means that your stock broker will be asked to sell it. If the company has the final word on the book, it probably means your broker will try to sell you the investment, especially if he isn't independent enough to tell his company "no."

Most (not all) large brokerage companies lay claim of ownership on the book. Such claims have been upheld in courts of law.

If, however, your broker lays claim to the book, he can recommend what he truly thinks is best for you. He's not under pressure to sell you investments simply because his company has to "move the stuff out".

Lets put it this way. If you trust the company more than you trust your broker, you will want the company to own the book. If on the other hand, you trust your individual broker and feel you can exert more influence over him than that billion dollar company with all of its conflicts, you would definitely want your broker to own the book.

Keep in mind however, that it is still *your* money. You own the book—at least your small piece of it. If you are fortunate enough to have a broker and a brokerage company that remembers who the *real* owners are, you'll be a happier client.

Ask your broker who owns his book.

How does your broker get his business?

7

How does your broker get his business?

Do you know a broker? Maybe he's a family member or a long time friend. An old high school buddy? Good. Do you really know him—or her? Are you part of his business? Is he *your* broker?

To a broker there are three types of people known to exist in the world. They are a client, a prospective client, or someone with no money at all, that will never be a client.

Prospective clients, or "prospects" as they are known in the business, are important to your broker. They are a potential name to be added to his book. Within the prospect category we could break it down a littler further. There are "family and friends" and their are "cold" Prospects.

Family and friends present certain quandaries to brokers. Different brokers handle their family and friends in different ways. Some brokers consider you family or friend first, prospect second. Others consider you a prospect first. Still others consider both of your relationships about equally, but make no mistake about it, you are still a prospect. Here's their quandary.

If your relative or friend happens to be a broker who is making constant decisions about something more important to most people than even their health, eventually something will go wrong. The investment simply won't work out. Out of all of those decisions and ideas he generates in a given day, week or month, your broker can only guarantee one thing to himself. Somewhere down the line, he is going to lose some money for his clients.

Hopefully if he is a good, conscientious broker he will make more money for his clients than he will lose, but eventually he will lose. It follows that when he loses someone's money, they are going to get upset. Sometimes they get real upset and fire him. Other times they get slightly upset and just don't want to talk to him. In either case when his client happens to be a good friend or family member, this little problem has devilish ways of compounding itself. It reaches out of his office and back to his family where his spouse or maybe even his children suffer from the conflict.

This problem becomes particularly acute when the broker's family member or friend knows little or nothing about investing and the risks that are involved. The problem does diminish significantly if the friend or family member is already a rather sophisticated and experienced investor. Experienced investors expect an occasional disaster along their path to investment success. The novice doesn't, no matter how many times the broker warns them.

You may not realize it but it is extremely difficult for your broker to call a client with bad news. It's *especially* difficult to call a good friend or family member and advise them that the great idea he recommended, just went squat.

For this reason many brokers hesitate to do business with their friends or family. They value the personal relationships far more than they value the few extra bucks they can earn from these clients. Other brokers either don't value the personal relationship as greatly, cannot afford to pass up the extra business, or in the case of the new broker, perhaps just haven't learned yet that the time will eventually come when the client will be upset.

For the new broker who recognizes that problems can and will happen, the dilemma is even greater. He hasn't developed the confidence in his own abilities that allow him to handle money comfortably. He may not want to use his friends or family as his guinea pigs, even though the extra business would mean a lot to him. He may refuse you altogether, noting that he doesn't wish to jeopardize the personal relationship. Respect him for his honesty. This person is truly a friend.

You are still a prospect, however, if you have investable dollars and your friend or family member happens to manage millions of dollars for a living.

He doesn't view you as a prospect because of his insatiable lust for control of your dollars, dollars he could add to his book. You are a prospect because of an even greater concern that your broker faces.

Any broker with over six days in the business has seen abuse of clients. Any broker knows how quickly an unethical or truly incompetent financial advisor can take advantage of, or unwillingly destroy a client's portfolio. An incompetent or unscrupulous broker can easily lead you to financial disaster or at the very least, to losses far above what would be considered normal risk. The broker who is your relative or friend does not want to see you become such a casualty. He may not want to jeopardize his personal relationship with you, but he certainly doesn't want you to get hurt, either. Thus his dilemma.

Does he accept you as his client knowing it could damage his personal relationship with you? Or does he refuse your business and by doing so, "throw you to the wolves?" At the very least he must always view you as something between a prospect and a client.

When your broker relative or friend views you as a potential client, he must also view you in an entirely different light. He will analyse you constantly to define in his broker's mind, what kind of client you would be.

If he accepts you as a client, a good understanding of his personal concerns will help you both. You can be assured that you will receive the best advice he can offer. You can also be assured he is a reasonably competent broker, totally comfortable with the advice that he offers. His greatest failure in dealing with you, may be that he handles your account too conservatively. Every so often, investors have to be very aggressive to make money in the financial markets and if your broker is not aggressive with you, it could cost you money.

If you ask your family member or friend to handle your investments for you, his response may be vague. He may also simply tell you he would prefer not to have you as a client. Don't get insulted. It simply means that he values his personal relationship with you far more than a business relationship. If he is a true friend, he will always be willing (and able) to offer you general advice if you ask for it. Contrary to the general rule, *his* free advice will probably be worth *far more than you paid for it!*

Here's a suggestion for families and friends who also happen to be considering a client-broker relationship. If the client (and of course, the broker) is a savvy investor, accept the relationship. Both partners will get a few chuckles from time to time over the losses that will inevitably take place, but will benefit from the gains realized. Certainly, the broker will be watching the account very closely as he does all of his really great clients. If, on the other hand, the client has little investment experience, the broker may wish to accept the account only on a primarily discretionary basis—with all of the appropriate warnings understood. In the discretionary relationship, the broker makes all investment decisions without consulting the client. Because of this, the broker doesn't have to make that hard call to his client every time a little something goes wrong. He is free to move in order to protect what really matters—the total balance of the account. If it works out, great. If not, both should feel free to cancel the relationship with no hard feelings. In any event, the broker will probably worry about this account more than any other because he now has the total responsibility for its performance.

Your broker is always trying to develop his "client/prospects". You may be one of them. You are the client that he already has, but he doesn't have all of your investment money. He may know this or he may not.

You have a broker. His name is Jerry. You have always given Jerry your little trades. You never mentioned to him that you had other money, your serious investments. You wanted to test Jerry out for a couple of years. Now you have some questions about the other investments. Jerry works for a large brokerage company and he's done quite well by you. You decide to give him a call.

"Hi Jerry, it's George. I need to talk to you about investing some more of my funds."

Jerry thinks to himself, "Another fifty shares of Bean Bag Distributors." He pokes the keys.

"Hmm, it's up to three and two teenths."

You quickly advise him that it's not Bean Bag that's on your mind today.

"That's not really why I'm calling, Jerry. I have about seven hundred in CD's and I'm getting a lousy return."

Jerry now settles back, wondering to himself, "Does he

mean seven hundred dollars or seven hundred thousand?"
He asks you. "Uh, okay, George, how much exactly?"

"About seven hundred thousand. I really don't know
exactly what to do with it. Could you give me some ideas?"

You, a client/prospect, have just become a client/client
for your broker. It took two years for you to develop enough
confidence in Jerry to ask him about your serious money.
But now you have. You have just developed from a casual
client, to a very significant client in Jerry's mind. One of
the best ways for a broker to get new business is by developing the "depth of his book". The money you place with
your broker goes into his book. The money you hold back,
is how "deep" his book really is. Your broker is always
wondering how deep his book really is. When your broker knows that you trust him with *all* of your money, you
are truly his most treasured and important client—no matter
how much money you have.

For your broker, the "cold prospect" is always out there
somewhere. It's the friend of a client, the friend of a friend,
a name in the phone book or the reverse telephone direc-
tory. Perhaps it's that couple out in the parking lot, nerv-
ously walking toward the door of his office.

Your broker has never met the cold prospect. This prospect may be a savvy person who has invested for years and
now needs a new broker, or it may be someone who has never
invested a dime.

For your broker, due in large part to government regulation (intervention?), marketing to the cold prospect is
very difficult. One of the reasons that you get so many cold
calls from brokers is that it's one of the few ways left for
them to acquire new clients, that is allowed by law.

Almost every piece of literature that your broker sends
to you in the mail, has to be approved by the Securities and

Exchange Commission (the SEC), or the National Association of Securities Dealers (NASD). For the sake of convenience, we are going to refer to both of these agencies col-
lectively and independently, as "Big Brother." Obtaining
these approvals is both costly and time consuming. In its
honorable quest to render the concept of "Caveat Emptor"
totally obsolete, Big Brother steps on an honest broker's
toes countless thousands of times. The recommendation of
specific investments therefore, is reduced in reality, to verbal
conversation with a licensed broker, usually followed by
formal prospectus. These prospectus' are written in legalese
and almost no one ever reads them. In situations when your
broker could easily send out a general mailing to alert you
to an idea you would want to pursue further, you must instead wait for his call. In the event that your broker can't
get to you, or perhaps doesn't even realize that you would
be interested in the idea, the opportunity is lost. Thank Big
Brother for the money you lose on investment ideas that
you never heard about. The cold prospect is also left out
in the dark, unable or unwilling to establish the verbal communication required to fully appreciate such opportunities.

Needless to say brokers and their companies strive to
fill this regulatory void.
Your brokerage company loves its cold call cowboys. Remember the broker who calls strangers from dawn till dusk?
His job is to acquaint cold prospects with the opportunities that are available to all. He calls you whether you are
interested, qualified to buy, or not. He calls you because it
is still one of the most successful ways of reaching those that
can and will, invest their money, if they know the right
opportunities exist.
Is cold calling efficient? Hardly. Two hundred calls might

produce two or three prospects. With luck one out of the two or three will actually purchase an investment. It may be annoying to the public but it's not very much fun for the broker, either. None of us like rejection and if you really want to know what rejection is like, try dialing strangers for ten hours straight about investing their money. The cold call cowboy's work is *hard work indeed*.

As you deal with your stock broker, you should know there probably isn't a broker alive today, that hasn't cold called at some point in his career. Most firms (including the largest ones) actually *force* their trainees to cold call strangers from telephone laboratories. The calls, and your responses, are *monitored by instructors*, who listen in. The minute you hang up, the instructors run over and critique the trainees on how they could have better persuaded you to buy.

Most brokers hate cold calling. Some flat out refuse to do it once they have become successful enough to survive without it. Others submit to it only when business is slow and they have to do something to survive. Still others will cold call as an adjunct to their normal prospecting routines. The "cold call cowboy" learns to live with it. Some of the cowboys even profess to enjoying it. Eventually they make cold calling the mainstay of their prospecting routine.

You may or may not like receiving those unsolicited calls but the next time you get one just remember. You can blame Big Brother! Big Brother has left cold calling as one of the very few ways for a broker to "legally" prospect—market if you will, for new business. And cold calling is one way your broker can get new business.

There are other ways to market to the cold prospect. Some brokers choose the "seminar" method. The public is invited to "investment seminars" either directly or by advertisement. Here too, the content of the seminar is strictly regulated. It is rare that you will hear much about a specific investment idea at a seminar. The seminar isn't about giving you specific recommendations. It's about building relationships. Depending on the speakers, seminars can be very interesting or brutally boring. If you want to discuss your personal finances however, you will most likely be invited to the broker's office for an appointment where he or she is legally allowed, through verbal communication, to discuss specifics with you. If you decide you feel comfortable enough with the broker to write a check, your broker has taken on more business.

Advertising, whether by the individual broker or by his company, is also very inefficient. Again, Big Brother must approve all media advertising. Most of the adds are very general in nature. Image stuff. Big Brother doesn't let your broker or his company get very specific. If, however, you should happen to be intrigued by one of those very general broker advertisements, your broker may bring you in as another client.

There are many other ways that the broker can prospect for business, but they're all about meeting you and forming a relationship so your needs can be addressed. Shopping Mall stands. Mailers (all approved by Big Brother). Some brokers have recently even taken up going door to door for business. It's probably a fair and viable way to meet cold prospects and get the word out—if the dog doesn't bite!

Two very important ways for the client to pick up new business and expand his book are "broker of the day" and "distributions".

When your broker is the broker of the day, he receives all of the calls from people who call in for information, or walk into the office without an appointment. As a client, you should never walk into a brokerage office without an appointment. When you do, you have absolutely no choice as to who you will receive as a broker. It could be a veteran with twenty years of experience or a trainee that just got out of broker school and hasn't yet met his first client. A brokerage company is not a bank. At a bank you don't expect to deal with the same person all of the time. You have absolutely no idea how much experience or lack thereof, the bank personnel have, and few would dare ask. A brokerage company is different.

Your relationship with a broker is personal. You can ask a broker about his qualifications. The broker you choose will always be your own personal broker. He will get to know you, your finances and your family. Every time you have a financial question, this is the person you are going to call. This person can generate wealth for you, or he can destroy you financially. Do you want to pick this person out of a hat?

Your broker also receives business (clients) from distributions. When a broker leaves the company, retires, or perhaps even dies, your account is distributed to the other brokers in the office. The manager simply collects your broker's book, and distributes the little pages (client accounts) as he sees fit. Suddenly you have a new broker, and the broker has new clients. Your broker gets instantly qualified clients and instantly lucrative new business during a distribution.

The single most important way that your broker gets new business however, is through the referrals of current clients. Nothing your broker can do to acquire new clients, compares to the business that can be brought in from his current clients who recommend him to their family or friends. If your broker is good enough to handle *your* investments, isn't he or she good enough to recommend to your closest associates? If you don't think your broker is at least that good, you better find yourself another broker.

The single best way to establish yourself as one of your

broker's very best clients is to refer other good clients like yourself. Even if your account consists of only five thousand dollars of a mutual fund that you will never sell, if you refer to your broker good clients, you will be a *good client* for life. And the business you refer to your broker, will be the best business he will ever receive.

Who does your broker work for?

8

Who does your broker work for?

Your broker has four choices. He can work for his company, he can work for himself, or he can work for you. That's three. The fourth choice is that he can try to work for all of the above.

If you happen to work for a corporation, your allegiance is usually to the corporation. If you are in business for yourself, your allegiance is to your own business and by default, your customers. If you are a professional you probably have primary allegiance to your clients, students, or patients.

In the brokerage industry it's not as simple. Your broker has to decide who it is he actually works for. Each of these three allegiances will conflict with each other on a continual basis.

Most brokers would say they are in business for themselves, even though they are in the employ of their brokerage companies. They would suggest that they are totally independent and able to offer their clients only what they personally feel is the best possible investment. Their true independence, however, depends largely on the company that they work for.

Some brokers determine early on that their true allegiance is to their company. The product that the company offers is always the best product and clients become mere customers; nameless faces that serve no meaningful purpose other than to purchase the company's product. The objective of these brokers is the same as their company's. Add profits to the bottom line.

These broker's have a short term objective and a longer one. First, they want to make a good living for themselves, as would anyone. Second, they want to move up the corporate management ladder in the hopes of securing an even better living for themselves.

If your broker's primary allegiance is to his company, it will manifest itself fairly quickly. Does he primarily consider your interests, or does he constantly try to "sell you" his company's latest product? Is he moving up through the management of his company, or has he continued to be a broker for longer than he or you can remember? Remember, in the brokerage business an associate vice president may not really be a management position. But a sales manager, or branch manager definitely is. If your broker is also a manager it isn't necessarily a bad thing. It may simply mean that he is truly dedicated not only to his clients but to the success of his company. Just remember that he may have two conflicting allegiances. In a good company it won't be much of a problem. In a company more interested in profits that client success, you may want to give your broker's promotion some serious thought.

If your broker's allegiance is to himself and his clients, you then have to look for signs of his independence. How independent does his company allow him to be?

Regardless of how your broker views his business, he does work for a company. What about that company? Who is it? Do you know them? Have you ever even heard of them? How do they rank? Among investors? With their brokers? How do they treat their clients? How do they treat their brokers?

As a client, you want to be able to answer these questions about your broker and his company. If you can answer all of these questions, and your answers satisfy you, you should be very comfortable with your broker. If there's even one of these questions you're unsure of, you better get sure about it. Nothing can affect the performance of your investment portfolio as much as the answers to these questions. Why? Because nothing can affect the performance of your investment portfolio as much as the *freedom your broker has*, to recommend only the investments he personally feels are best for you.

If your broker is very knowledgeable and very independent, and he works for a company that thinks it owns him, your broker has a serious problem—and so do you. If your broker feels he needs constant guidance, research and support, he had better be working for a firm that provides it. If you place more trust in your broker than the company he or she works for, your broker had better own that book. If you are investing with a stranger for the first time and look primarily at the name of the company for your comfort, it might be better if the company owns the book. If your brokerage company trusts its brokers and treats them well, they will be more comfortable with the broker owning the book. If not, you can bet the company owns the book.

Here are some things to look for. Perhaps some insight will allow you to come up with some of the answers to these tricky little questions that you may have never thought of before.

In the ideal world you trust your broker implicitly. You feel your broker's allegiance is to you. You've been dealing with him for years. You rely solely on his investment advice and by default would allow him the choice of his company affiliation. That's the ideal world. Now for the real one.

In the real world you trust your broker but the fact that

you know quite a bit about his company doesn't hurt the relationship. In the real world you haven't been dealing with your broker for years. You may even be searching out a broker for the very first time. You will definitely feel more comfortable knowing that the company he works for, is an established and reputable firm. They pick and screen their brokers and hire only the best, most proficient and caring talent they can find. You rely on the company's reputation. You assume that they would never jeopardize that reputation by hiring anything but the best brokers. This may be a valid assumption but remember. The company's idea of "best broker", may not be the same as yours. They are interested in commissions. You are more concerned with the performance of your account.

There are many different styles of brokerage companies. Even within the same company, offices and their managers may have different styles. Different companies allow different margins of independence to your broker.

The large national wirehouse is where most brokers and for that matter, most clients, begin. The term "Wire house" developed because the companies used to "wire" (telegraph) their stock buys and sells to their traders on the floors of the stock exchanges. A client walked into his broker's office in Peoria. He told the broker to buy him 500 shares of "whatever" stock. The broker then wrote out a "buy" ticket with all of the pertinent information on it, sent it to his "wire room," and the order was wired to an exchange where a trader actually purchased the shares for you. The trader then wired back a confirmation of the trade to the broker, and the client owned 500 shares of "whatever".

You know these companies by their more informal designation. "Old, large and *very well known*".

A new broker doesn't have a book. He needs training. He needs maximum support. He doesn't know enough about investments or the business to even begin thinking about independence. More importantly, he needs all of those brand spanking new clients that only a big, well known company name will bring in.

The beginning client doesn't know much about investment brokers or in many cases, very much about investing. Where else is he going to go? To some small little shop he's never heard of? And deal with a broker he knows nothing about? It's not very likely.

Doing business with a well known company would sound like a sure thing, right? Well - - -! Not necessarily in the brokerage industry. The big national brokerage house is Big Business, period. Please note the capital "B's." Their business is a business of commission dollars and make no mistake about it, that's where they focus.

When it comes to your broker's independence, the big company can take advantage of the power they possess, and to your broker the word "advantage" is spelled "P R E S S U R E".

That big business is under immense pressure to perform. That pressure passes from the shareholders, to the board of directors, down the line through the various levels of management, right into your broker's lap. As with any big business it becomes a political pressure cooker as the lower level managers strive to meet the numbers that will get them the promotions that will subject them to even greater pressure and hopefully compensate them for it.

"So what" you say. "What does that mean to me as a client?"

Remember that broker we talked about, the one fighting for his office at the end of the year? That's what it means to you as a client. If your broker is under intense pressure to sell enough of a proprietary fund (a mutual fund owned and operated by the brokerage company) to win the latest sales contest or at least curry a little favor from the management, you the client, are definitely going to hear about that fund—whether it's good or bad. Maybe it's a Limited Partnership with a seven percent commission that you never even knew you paid, as opposed to a stock at two percent or a fund at four or five. Yup, you'll hear about it. Count on it.

At what rate does the company pay out commission to its brokers? The greater the payout, the less pressure your broker is under to at least "make ends meet." If you the client, are paying the same commission for an investment purchase, would you prefer your broker to get a fair share of it or would you rather most of it be swallowed up by that big political pressure cooker?

Let me ask the question a different way. Who do you think you exert more influence over? The individual broker you personally deal with day in and day out, or his big company?

In the last chapter we touched briefly on two of the most important ways that your broker gets his new business. They were "broker of the day", and "distributions". Lets explore them in more detail. Lets see how the company can use them to pressure your broker into doing what they want him to do. Lets see how they can relieve your broker of his independence.

Broker of the day is kind of fun for your broker. You will recall this is when a prospect either calls or walks into the office without any previous contact. Usually it's to sell thirty two shares of stock or maybe buy a single share of a favorite company for a child's birthday party or something. Not very much business there. Not much commission.

On occasion, however, fifty or even five hundred thousand dollars walks in the door needing some help. Your broker definitely wants to be the broker of the day when that happens. Broker of the day can bring in very serious business from time to time. The brokerage company can *take away* "broker of the day" from any broker they are unhappy with, for *any* reason. If your broker didn't sell his quota of the last thing the company wanted sold, he can lose his broker of the day privileges. It can cost him money.

Distributions are rarer but even better. When another broker in the office retires, quits, leaves the company or dies, he may leave a book of millions of dollars that "instantly" needs to be serviced.

The book is "distributed" to the remaining brokers in the office or at least within the firm. This is an instant production (pay) increase to the receiving brokers. The distribution is discretionary though. There may or may not be a policy on it but when push comes to shove, the management has total discretion as to who gets what distribution.

Your broker does not want to be coming up short in the company's latest sales contest, when his fellow broker's Mercedes has a run in with a Mack truck on the boulevard—and loses. There's a thirty million dollar *distribution* about to happen. If your broker is not doing his part to sell the company's latest favorite investment, he may not get a dime of that distribution. Remember the investment banking side of the business?

"What's that got to do with me as a client?" you ask?

Everything. When ABC Pizza Pie, Inc. agrees to pay XYZ brokerage company to bring out their stock so that they can pay off their crippling loans to DEF bank and maybe turn a profit sometime in the next decade, XYZ brokerage has a problem. They have to "move" the stock. Someone has to buy it. That little effort usually ends up in the laps of the "sales force" otherwise known as "your broker". The lousier the issue? The more pressure on the sales force to move it out. Guess who gets a call so your broker is in good graces with his management, when distribution time comes. Is your phone ringing?

Not all big brokerage companies operate this way. Some of the national firms don't even have their own mutual funds. Not all offices in the ones that do, play by the company's rules. Not all brokers do.

Branch offices and individual brokers can usually refuse to sell investments they don't like, if their books are big enough—if they have enough power and independence. But bigger firm is not always better firm and if your broker is under these kinds of pressures, beware. Your portfolio may not look like you want it to. It probably won't even look like your broker wants it to because he is not always at liberty to offer you the investments that he likes.

Another kind of brokerage company is the "penny shop." We're not going to spend a lot of time here on the penny shop. It suffers from dubious reputation.

Whether reputable or not, this company specializes in very cheap stocks—stocks often selling for less than a dollar. Thus the term "penny stock" or "penny stock shop." It shouldn't come as any surprise that it's a lot easier to convince a large number of investors to spend a few dollars, than it is to convince a few investors to commit substantial dollars to serious investments. Some penny stocks are good investments. Many large and successful companies started out being penny stocks. But the abuses in the business are rampant. The Government simply can't keep up with policing the various schemes and we couldn't begin to list them all here. High pressure sales combined with low or no performance stocks might sum it up. You throw your dice? You take your chances.

If you want to buy a penny stock, buy it from a broker you know, that works for a company that you know. Never buy a stock you never heard of, from a broker or brokerage company that you have never heard of. This may sound like simple advice, but you would be amazed how often people ignore it.

The "boutique brokerage" is an interesting firm. These firms and their "regional" cousins usually develop to service a specific area or locality. Unlike their national counterparts they develop an expertise in a certain locality, or perhaps a particular type of investment, choosing to expand or not to expand as their management sees fit. Often but not always they "clear" through another firm. This means that they rely on another firm to execute their trades on the exchanges. They many not be large enough to handle those functions themselves. This isn't necessarily a bad thing.

The boutique is to brokerage what the corner deli is to grocery stores. They may not have every investment you are looking for. You may have to run to the larger firm once in a while to get what you want, but if you like dealing in a highly personalized environment, if your boutique is a good one, and if you have you have a high comfort level with your individual broker, a boutique or a regional firm can be a very nice place to do business.

You can also deal with an independent broker. Like many of the boutiques and regionals your independent also clears through another firm. He relies on that firm not only to clear transactions but usually to provide the other basic services you require such as statements and tax reporting.

Another type of independent is the fee based money manager. This person may or may not be a registered investment broker (the one licensed to receive commissions for executing securities trades) but he should be a registered investment advisor. This money manager usually charges a set fee on the assets he manages—between one and two percent is common. If you place your money with him to be managed, he takes total discretion. He will not, nor is he required to call you every time he buys and sells a security for your account. When he buys or sells a security for you and his other clients, he does so through another brokerage company licensed to do so—and they get paid the commissions. Since he is the advisor, he need not pay full service commissions and since he often buys in bulk (larger quantities of securities which he then splits into his various accounts) he will usually receive a less expensive rate. Often you will find an independent operating in both the capacity of broker and fee based manager. It does offer him and his clients flexibility in the management of the accounts. Some clients prefer to pay commissions, thereby paying only for the securities actually bought or sold—or pay on a "transaction basis" as it is more eloquently called. Others feel that by paying their advisor on a straight fee basis it eliminates the pressure on the advisor to do business simply to generate commissions. Both systems have very distinct advantages and disadvantages but there is definitely something to be said for at least having the choice. We'll delve deeper into the pro's and con's of these two different money management styles in our chapter on "Managed Money."

Regardless of how he manages money, this financial pro is exactly what his name implies. He is fiercely "independent." He's in business for himself. He relies entirely on himself, perhaps with one or two close associates, to determine what investments are best for his clients. He answers to no one but his clients.

Almost no broker starts off as an independent. Usually the independent broker has come from one of the other environments. He then struck out on his own. He is no longer willing or able to operate in the environment of the larger company. Be careful here. There are two general types of independent brokers.

The first is a seasoned pro, most capable of servicing your account in a highly proficient manner. He usually has years of experience in the business, has a substantial client base, and has simply elected to operate his business with total autonomy.

The second independent broker is the one who simply couldn't make it at the larger firm. With inherited or borrowed money, he opened his own office in a last ditch attempt to survive in the business. He may or may not be good. He may or may not succeed. You won't know until he either does or doesn't.

One rule obviously prevails when dealing with the independent. You must be absolutely and completely comfortable with the competence of your broker. You have to be. There's no one else there! He doesn't have a large company to fall back on, when questions arise that he can't answer. If you happen to have a good independent broker you can be sure of one thing. You will get superb service and totally objective investment advice. This broker works for no one but you.

We now see that your broker works for himself. He works for his company. He also works for his clients. We have looked at some of the different types of companies. We have seen some of the ways those companies can influence their brokers. Knowing these things, how can you, the client, go about finding (or be comfortable in keeping) that perfect broker? The one that is willing, able, and most importantly *allowed by his company*, to keep your best interests at heart?

It's simple really. You have to educate yourself. Now you know what to look for. *Look for it.*

Talk to people that are happy with their brokers and the companies that they work for. Are these people comfortable? Have they done well? If so, you are off to a good start. Even they, though, may not be able to answer all of the questions about broker relationships that you now want answered. Most clients, happy or otherwise, have no idea what goes on in the broker's world. So don't stop looking.

Keep watching for signs of independence in your broker. Does he always follow the company line? Has he ever said something like, "Fred, it's like this. My company seems to absolutely love this stock, but I'm not totally comfortable with it. I really think that maybe we should watch it for awhile before we buy."

Ask your broker about his company. Is your broker honest about it? Does he give you the typical "great company, love this place" line, or does he give it to you straight, listing the good with the bad? Can he back up the good with independent information? Does he *sweat* when you ask him the questions?

Finally, do some research. I don't mean to run right out to the stationary store and grab the latest copy of any financial magazine, but do keep your eyes and ears open. If you happen to catch a magazine or newspaper article rating the brokerages, *tune in*. There may be good information in there. Don't be like every one else and immediately focus on the commission rankings. Look for the *really important* stuff. What is the pressure on the broker. It's often there rated in black and white—you just never knew to look for it or to care about it. It was the broker's problem not yours. Are they in and out of law suits every week or do they tend to have a pretty clean record? How do their clients rate the company? Are they happy? Are they satisfied? Do they have their own mutual funds? Do they pay their brokers more to sell their own funds?

Pay special attention to any article that asks *brokers* to rate their companies. Clients may be happy with the companies but the brokers are the ones that really know. If they really love their companies it will show in the rankings. If they've got a beef, it too, will come out in the survey. Brokers love to improve their companies and unfortunately it's a lot easier to do it anonymously through the press, than through the management chain. Grab a copy of Registered Representative if you can, when they rate the brokerages. Registered Representative is a trade magazine for brokers. The public doesn't get a peek at it very often. You may not even be able to get a copy of it but your broker has one. Ask him how his company came out in the annual ranking. If his company did well, he'll be happy to show it to you. If he doesn't have a copy or a reprint quickly available, it's probably telling you something.

Watch for basic changes in the way your broker does his or her business. If your broker has always avoided certain types of investments and suddenly calls you with one of them that's just too good to refuse, you may want to refuse. One call may only mean that he has found a better idea or that, perhaps the markets have changed and caused him to reconsider. If, on the other hand, he suddenly seems to be *constantly* changing his investment philosophy, take note. Your guy or gal could be under the gun.

You don't have to be paranoid. But being alert can't hurt you. You and your broker will have a far better relationship if you both understand where he's coming from.

Finally, make a simple call. (800) 289-9999. Your broker's record of licensing problems are a matter of public record. This telephone number is the National Association of Securities Dealers' (NASD) public line. They have your broker and his record of complaints on computer. Have handy your broker's name, company and the branch office that he works in, pick up the phone and dial. It's a free two minute call that could save you some really big headaches.

Does your broker have the right tools?

9

Does your broker have the right tools?

I occasionally ask clients and prospective clients a question. "When you make money in the markets where do you think that money comes from?" Innocent enough question isn't it?

Most experienced investors know that you make money in the financial markets by *taking it from somebody else.*

If you are going to take some one else's money in the financial markets, *you had better have the tools to do it with.* There's a lot of very big money out there in those markets and those very big players don't like other people taking their money from them.

Investing is a business of knowledge. In the investment business, *information* is what knowledge is all about. Information is smart. Information is critical. You can be the most brilliant person in the world but if you don't have good information immediately available to you—at your finger tips, somebody who does is eventually going to come along and take away your money.

As you merrily perform heart surgery during the day or perhaps teach your history class at school, you might want to take some comfort in knowing that your broker is hard at work watching over your account, gathering, processing and interpreting the volumes of information that he had better have access to. This is one of the most important reasons for having a broker in the first place.

When a broker settles in to his easy chair at night to catch up on the television news and/or read the evening newspaper, what he sees and reads had very well better be "old news" if it pertains in any way, to the millions of dollars he's responsible for investing. His idea of "old news" as it pertains to investing money, is something that happened fifteen minutes ago.

To access and process this information, to have this knowledge, your broker had better have the right tools. He had better know how to use them swiftly and efficiently, or somebody out there is going to be tapping buckaroos out of his book. Someone is going to be taking *your* money!

There are basically two sources your broker has to gather and process information. What his company provides him with, and what he provides himself with.

There are two categories of information available. Old news with deeper analysis and current news with rapid analysis.

Most if not all major companies today provide their brokers with volumes of analysis. And I do mean volumes. Your broker could rent out the local library, gut it, throw out every piece of written matter in it, and refill it in about two months with the volumes of information he gets from his company.

Most brokers cannot even begin to digest it all. If your broker is not a pretty good speed reader he can't even digest a small part of it. The concern is not whether or not there is enough analysis. The concern is how to sift through it all, and screen it for what is relevant. Your broker has this problem, *big time.*

In addition to analysis, your broker needs the current news. He needs to know what's happening, while it's happening—not ten or fifteen minutes later. If Donald Dud, a nationally followed financial columnist and network "know-it-all" comes out on television at two fourteen in the afternoon, to dump all over your largest holding, you want your broker to know about it. He may or may not do anything about it, but he had better know about it and be able to assess the potential damage.

To respond to this need for instant information most brokerage companies provide two sources of information. The first is news retrieval on the quote screen. That same screen that constantly updates your broker with stock quotes can also provide news updates from various sources. Various firms provide this news in various degrees. Some firms provide only news headlines on the broker's screen. They might have separate terminals somewhere in the office that the broker can run to, to get all of the juicy the details beneath the headlines. Other firms provide each broker with the detailed news at his or her own screen.

Some companies punish their brokers, by reducing such informational services to the broker, if the broker doesn't make a sales quota or two. What a nice thing for them to do to *your* money. Regardless of the convenience, the news should be available to your broker when it breaks.

The second source of information is instant communication with company headquarters, where they have even more information available. Almost every major brokerage office today, is hooked up to its headquarters by satellite and what is commonly referred to as a "squawk box." This is simply a speaker that the broker listens to during the day. If hot news breaks out somewhere, and company headquarters feels the need to get that news to its brokers, they simply pick up a phone and start hollering. Their comments are fired off to the satellites and are instantly transmitted back to satellite dishes which sit on the roofs of every branch office in the country.

A broker in Podunk, Idaho gets the same message as a broker in Los Angeles or New York City, from the little speaker boxes which sit on or near their desks. They all get it at the same time. Many companies also have the system hooked into television monitors so brokers in a branch can gather around the set after the market closes, and watch the company gurus decipher the latest breaking situations.

One company I know of takes the concept even further. It has *two way* communication. At any moment during the day their brokers can pick up a telephone, squeeze the transmitter, and broadcast a question to both their headquarters and every other branch office within the company. The broker's question and the answer received, can be heard by every other broker on the system. If the broker should see something going on with one of his stocks that he needs to know more about, he's literally an instant away from his company's chief technician, fundamental analyst, chief economist, or anyone else he needs to talk to. Every other broker in the system hears the question, is alerted to the issue, and receives the same answer. If necessary, the broker can then call his clients—often before news is more than two minutes old.

Important events affecting any given investment, are also immediately transcribed and flashed onto each broker's quote machine. If the broker was otherwise occupied when the event occurred, the information is available to him immediately, when he or she is ready to receive it. Your broker doesn't get his business news the same way you do. By the time the news appears in the paper, *it's ancient history*.

The broker's quote machine is truly his "tool of the trade." The quote machine allows your broker to monitor stock trades instantly, as they occur, not fifteen or twenty minutes later like the television or many stock computer services do. Not only does the machine show the trade the instant it's recorded, it also shows the volume of trades for a stock at the given moment. It also shows what is called the "size". Size, simply defined, is the volume of the offers and the bids for a stock.

If a broker pokes in a stock symbol on the quote machine, it looks something like this:

<u>IBM</u> 63 1/8 B 63 1/8 A 63 3/8 20 X 500 LT 500 11:06
H 63 7/8 L 63 AH 74 1/8 AL 51 PE 12.6 Yld3.2

From this information you should easily be able to determine that the last trade for IBM took place at 11:06 for 63 1/8, was probably a sell, and was for 500 shares. The current size is 2,000 shares offering to buy at 63 1/8 while 50,000 shares are willing to sell at 63 3/8. A few minutes of watching the size change, will probably confirm that this stock is under sell pressure. If you want to buy it, you should wait a few minutes. The 2,000 to buy will probably disappear. You can probably get the stock for $63.00 flat—or even less if the selling continues.

By watching the volume, size and general action of a stock for only a few moments, your broker can usually determine whether the market is buying or selling the stock in question.

You simply can't measure the money your full service broker can save you by simply "holding the order" until you gain a quarter to a half point on your trade. Usually he won't even remember to mention it to you. Why can he save you this money? Because he has the right information at his finger tips.

In addition to the news and stock quotes, the quote machine supplies your broker with client account information. He can call up your account and give you its value constantly. Most firms update account information daily. Some even update it during the day.

Your broker's quote machine also provides him with information on various bond inventories (bonds the company has in its inventory for sale to clients) and a host of other items of information. In short, your broker's quote machine is his connection to the outside world.

All of these different features on the machine are incremental. Different machines have different capabilities. And each of those individual capabilities cost your brokerage company money. Make sure your broker has a good quote machine. And make sure his company doesn't barter those features, in an effort to pressure him into doing things he might not want to do. Without good information, your broker doesn't know any more about the current status of the markets than you do.

Your broker has another very important informational input. There are other brokers in his office. If your broker happens to be sleeping at the switch when some unusual news item breaks, chances are there's going to be some quick and lively conversation in the office to wake him up. Every broker in a good office, is the client *and* the broker of every *other* broker in the office. None of these people are hesitant to share ideas or events with each other. Almost all brokers try to help and inform their fellow brokers.

If broker George in the next office hears something of interest, he pops his face into his neighbor's office to share it. If his fellow broker didn't happen to hear it, she still receives the information. George tells her what was going on. If necessary, she can then call her clients to tell them about it. Information is shared between brokers and it is shared freely. You as a client can only benefit from this fast-paced knowledgeable discourse between men and women who, each in their own way, are always finely tuned to the markets and the events surrounding them.

Many brokers accept the tools offered by their companies and then go a few steps further. Many brokers have purchased their own computers because the company doesn't offer one. Sure, the company provides the quote screens. Depending on the company, there are various levels of embellishments on the systems. But to really have it all, many brokers use their own personal computers. A broker doesn't have to rely on the company as much, when he has his own machine.

Your broker's computer may have a program that contains all of his client's holdings. If so, he can run profit and loss statements for any of his client's, on any given day. He can run Schedule D reports (information on profits and losses for tax returns) any time he wants to. He has client information and notes instantly available to him, together with client telephone numbers which his computer can dial automatically. If he wants to talk to a client again in eight days, his computer won't let him forget about it. If a client needs information, the request goes into his computer and the client's name keeps popping up in front of him until the request is answered.

Such a broker would have information on almost every mutual fund that exists, on his computer. If someone calls him and needs to know the beta (risk measurement) and return on XYZ mutual fund, his machine will give them the answer in about thirty seconds. He can bring up a chart on most stocks in fifteen seconds and the rest of them in about two minutes if he has to. Are you dealing with a broker whose only access to a stock chart is the same two week old chart book that you have? A chart, is a picture of a stock (or fund's) performance. If your broker is relying on a three week old picture of your stock in today's fast moving investment world, good luck.

Can your broker give you a daily picture of your profits, losses and tax picture if you need it, in thirty seconds? Can he analyse over five thousand mutual funds in a couple of minutes before your very eyes?

Does your broker have a computer? Does he or she have the systems necessary to provide the information you require? Does your broker have immediate access to his or her headquarters from the satellite squawk box? Does he have news retrieval? The analytical reports and information? Does he or she have the experience to efficiently utilize all of those tools while still operating the most powerful tool of all, his or her brain?

Does your broker have the information and experience necessary to take that money from other investors while keeping your money where it belongs; in your account.

Even the best of brokers won't be able to win for you all of the time. But without good information, without the experience and the expertise, *without the tools*, you don't stand a chance.

Regardless of the tools they have, brokers like all of us, are made up of different personalities. Different brokers operate their businesses with different styles. Lets take a look at some of the different types of brokers. Do you recognize one of these brokers? Is he or she your broker?

The Salesman.

10

The Salesman

"It's a good idea not to be too smart in this business. If you're too smart you'll never sell anything."

Is this the creed of the broker salesman? Since brokerage companies thrive on the commissions a salesman can produce, has it also become the creed of many a brokerage company?

I can't tell you how many times this has been told to people, during their careers as investment brokers. If a broker thinks too much about the investments that he places his clients in, he weeds out around eighty percent of the opportunities, and works only with the rest. He weeds out a lot of commission opportunities in the process. If, on the other hand, he's "not too smart" (or simply don't care), he *doesn't* think about them. He simply hops on the phone and sells any investment that is given to him, to anyone who will buy. A broker can make lots of money selling whatever comes his way. A broker can become a "super star" producer. But when the investment takes its inevitable flop, *clients lose money*. The purely sales oriented broker is willing to "blow up" clients without a second thought. What's a "blow up"? If the broker loses his clients twenty five to eighty five percent of their money inside of two weeks (or maybe two days), it's a "blow up." A salesman doesn't worry about blowing up his clients. A salesman worries about his *production*.

"Don't try to be too smart in this business."

It may first be told to the broker in his manager's office, discussing why the broker's production isn't quite up to speed. It is often said at sales meetings.

For years, a broker I know, suffered, never willing to respond to such comments. After all. The salesmen were right. They were bringing down a hundred fifty, maybe two hundred thousand, maybe more. This broker was scraping by with sixty to a hundred thousand, depending on the given year. While he was struggling to pay bills, the super stars were buying Corvettes and boats. If your broker is really smart and cares about you, you can probably rest assured that he screens his investment ideas and is not making a fortune in his chosen field—at least not on commissions.

One night after another surf and turf sales meeting, the broker was fed up. Introduced to yet another "sales star" as someone he should idolize and try to emulate, he was forced to listen as the sales star discussed in vague detail, his latest sales ideas. The investments that Super Star was selling, paid high commissions. But if one thought about them for over a nano-second, one could quickly see how the investments could lose money, big time.

The salesman soon detected from the broker's grimaces and obvious boredom, that he was totally unimpressed. Finally the broker's lack of interest and failure to drool over Super Star's brainstorms began to get to the hero.

"You can't be too smart in this business. Smart people don't make any money."

The broker couldn't take it. "I know" he replied. "Smart people treat their client's money like it's their own. They do what's right for their clients."

The super star huffed off with his "not too smart" tail tucked between his legs. The broker's circle of conscientious broker friends smiled wryly at Super Star's abrupt departure, but they all knew it was an empty victory. Smart brokers have to work hard to hold on to their money, and the money of their clients. "Super star doesn't." If the hot shot blows away a few thousand of his own money because of his ignorance or stupidity, it doesn't matter to him. He's bringing home fifteen to twenty thousand a month in commissions. He needn't care. If he blows up a few clients, new ones are just three or four hundred cold calls away. The intellect is the smart guy? Super Star is the winner!

If you buy the salesman, you buy the company line. This guy doesn't get too involved with details or the mechanics of whether an investment is good or not. Having passed the series 7 test (which may have been an effort), he is quite willing to let the company do his thinking for him. The company is more than happy to assume this role. The salesman's job is to "bring in the money." The company will decide for him, how to invest it.

There is not an investment product for sale that doesn't come complete with a "script." A script is a canned dialogue designed to highlight the salient points of an investment for those who haven't the capability to think it through for themselves. The script usually comes complete with all of the answers to any investor objections that would ever come up.

All the salesman has to do is memorize the script and the answers to the objections. In fifty cold calls he'll find someone who will cave in and buy.

The salesman will get offended if you are resourceful enough to come up with some reason not to buy, that's not covered in his script. He may even get obnoxious if you have the nerve to tell him flat out that you're not interested. I have actually heard some of these people call back a number that hung up on them.

"I wasn't finished talking to you. Did we get disconnected?"

"No, jackass, I hung up on you!"

Any "buy signal" will do for a salesman. A "buy signal" is anything you say or do to indicate your interest. A simple way to tell if a strange broker really has your best interest in mind, is to *test him* with a buy signal. Think of a completely hopeless investment. Then ask him about it. Express your interest in possibly acquiring just such a jewel. A broker with your best interest in mind, will instantly suggest you reconsider. The salesman will instantly think of ten to twenty reasons why you should make the investment. Then he will ask you for your order.

Do you want this charming fellow to be your broker? You might.

The company line he's selling may not be a bad one. If the salesman broker is calling from a name brand outfit, and you are interested in what he's offering, it might not be a bad deal. This individual may not be concerned as to whether you win or lose. He may not even be capable of hazarding a guess as to how the investment will work out. But a reputable company can't afford to jeopardize their reputation too often.

How does the salesman broker make money? He does make it. He makes a lot of it. Three words sum it up—charm, flattery and persuasiveness.

What makes someone buy something as important as an investment from a perfect stranger over the phone? It's certainly not a deep intellectual thought process. It's probably not even an understanding of the product. Oh sure, there may be a light hearted attempt to discuss and define what the investment is all about, but that's not the issue.

Unless you refuse his advances this guy is charming with a capital "C." He'll ask about your wife, your wench, your kids, your puppy dogs, and even express profound inter-est in your favorite hobby if you show just the vaguest in-terest in what he is hawking.

He can be flattering too. Here you are, at seven thirty at night. Your wife is out at the local PTA meeting, and your three offspring are out on the town making life miserable for the local constabulary. You decide to hit the recliner to take in a television show. You plop the wireless telephone down on the table beside you so you don't have to get up unless it's the cops. Just as you start to relax over the evening newspaper the dreaded phone interrupts you.

"Hello?"

"Good evening, sir. My name is Harry Jones, and I'm with Fernwell, Fernwell and RinkyDink investment brokers. I'm calling you this evening to introduce myself and de-termine whether you might be a candidate for an exciting but *very* conservative investment opportunity that we are currently offering, with an excellent potential for tax de-ferred returns." You're almost out of breath now just from listening to the guy, but he continues. "Do you currently have any Cds or money markets that are earning you less that ten/eight/six percent a year?" He finally inhales.

Whatever his question, it will be structured so that you cannot possibly answer without a "Yes" unless you have ab-solutely no money at all.

"Uh, Yeah."

"Great! Do you currently have at least five thousand dol-lars that you would be able to invest if the opportunity was right for you?" If you don't the conversation will be brief.

As the voice on the other end of the phone rambles on, you start thinking.

"Gee, I do have that seven thousand in the bank and it's not doing much. Here's this really important investment broker calling me with a great idea." A chill of excitement ripples down your spine. "I didn't even know a guy like me could invest."

He continues. "Doesn't that sound great? All I need is your okay and a check in three days, and I can get you right into this."

"Well, gee, it sounds good, but I better talk it over with my—"

"Gee sir, that's okay. But I don't know if I'll have any left by tomorrow. I'm sure you make important decisions every day without your wife. This could be one of them. I'm sure she'll be as excited as you are over the potential of this."

"Well, great. Where do I send the check?"

This broker is persuasive. He can think of more reasons for you to feel warm and comfortable with his idea than you can possibly imagine. You buy because you are convinced that this is the best possible idea to make money, that you have ever heard of.

Does all of this sound a little absurd? Perhaps, but it happens over and over again. This buyer wasn't sold on the investment. He was sold on the idea that the broker thought enough of him to call him and explain such an opportunity. He was convinced after the call, that almost nothing could go wrong with the investment. He never invested before. He didn't even know he *could* invest! It didn't take the salesman long to realize it either. This guy was simply flattered to death.

When his lady dragged herself in from the PTA meeting he couldn't wait to tell her what he had done. When he told her—well, that's another story.

There's another kind of person that the salesman can get a positive response from. The savvy investor with money.

This person loves investing in different things, and usual-ly keeps an extra twenty to fifty thousand liquid in case a good opportunity comes along. He realizes that not every firm has every product and, if caught at the right time in the right mood, he might be willing to listen. If the script is interesting, his years of investment experience will usu-ally fill in the gaps. He can get an idea of the general con-cept. He probably knows more about the investment than the salesman before the conversation is over. If he likes the idea, he'll drop five or ten in it. He has eight to twelve bro-kerage accounts anyway. What's one more?

In any case, if the investment company that is making the offering is a reputable one, the investor probably wins over time. It would have to be a really poor investment idea, not to outperform a CD over three or four years.

One final thought. All stock brokers are salesmen. You may have an excellent broker who happens to be a poor salesman. This can work to your detriment because he won't be able to convince you of his very good ideas. You may find a very good salesman who is a very poor broker. This of course, isn't a good thing. You may also find a superb bro-ker, who just happens to be a great salesman too. Lucky you!

The Intellect.

11

The Intellect

This is one broker that really knows investing. This broker works hard at his craft and he wants his clients to be impressed with his knowledge. They should be impressed. This broker truly does possess a wealth of knowledge in all of the various political, economic, and sociological pieces of the increasingly complex investment puzzle.

Look for this broker out on the board room floor. He's the opposite of the salesman. For all of his efforts, he may well make less than half the commissions of the salesman. Where the company places his desk, (in an office or on the floor) is determined by his commission production, not his investment ability. Keep in mind, however, that the intellect may very well be making as much money from his own investments, as he does from his earned commissions.

If you happen to catch your intellect broker without an appointment, you will probably find him feverishly studying the latest events in Bangkok or three quarters of the way through his sixth investment prospectus of the day.

This in fact, may be one of the few people in the world who can actually read *and understand* a prospectus. A prospectus is a summary of a new investment or issue. Many people try to read them, particularly "do-it-yourself" investors, but few can accurately measure the risk/reward potential. Lawyers write these things. Lawyers are by nature and training, instinctively risk-averse. Therefore, they write the prospectus' in language that would frighten off Attila the Hun.

Your intellect knows this and, reading between the lines, he analyzes the *real* risks of the investment. He gleans from the package what he needs to know to make a decision.

It's usually a knowledgeable and well thought out decision. When this broker integrates the information in the prospectus with his own knowledge of the investment world, and his clients' risk tolerances, the client will usually get a sterling investment.

Don't try to determine whether you have an intellect broker from the his past occupations or callings. Being an intellect in the financial world is not necessarily about formal education. It's about *informal* education. It's about educating one's self. This broker's basic smarts allow him to constantly digest new and changing information and constantly changing information is what the investment world is all about.

Just because this broker sits out on the floor with the lower producers, don't write him off as inexperienced. The opposite is more often the case. The intellect usually puts his own money where his mouth is. There is no better way to gain experience in the investment world, than to invest your own money. Sure he'd love to have his own office. But it doesn't bother him much. His real office is between his ears. He really doesn't care too much about the trappings.

The intellect broker may be out on the floor, but make no mistake about it, he's important to the office. This is the "broker's broker", the guy all the other brokers bounce ideas off of. He's the guy they ask for explanations. They always question him.

"You're buying what?! The Ripmobile subordinated 12 3/4's of "02 at 38? Rated DDZ? Are you out of your mind?"

Our intellect has found some junk (poor quality) bonds that yield 12 3/4 percent on the original $1,000 face value. Because the company issuing them is in poor financial shape, the general market figures the company will never be able to pay them off. The bonds are now priced at only $380 per thousand. They are, however, still paying $127.50 in interest, and at the purchase price of $380 the yield is about 33 percent. If the company goes bankrupt, all the money is lost. However if the company recovers, the investor eventually gets the interest plus the $1,000 face value. The intellect, with a wry smile on his face, quietly enlightens his challenger.

"Well, they're callable at 101 ($1,010) in six months. Ripmobile just came out with a new fuel system that gets seventy miles a gallon off of a four hundred horsepower engine. They just took the patent to a consortium and already have the money to pay for these bonds, committed to them at seven percent. I'll ride 38 to 101 in six months any day, especially if I'm getting paid 33 percent to wait."

"Oh. Uhm, any left?"

There are a couple of different ways to use your intellect broker. If you like to try to eliminate all risk or uncertainty before you lay down your buckaroos, you will ask him to explain every detail.

He will, right down to how the Ripmobile's new fuel injector with variable pulsating interlocking internal air mixture sensing and combustion anticipatory individually-imbedded microchip circuitry allows it to drain over ninety eight point six two seven percent of allowable BTU content from the newly-developed but easily producible ultra-delineated octane fuel it uses.

Once you have been fully educated as to how quickly

the new fuel will become available and the estimated cost to benefit value of the new system, you will plunk down all the extra money you can come up with, on those junk bonds.

You will buy because the whole thing makes sense to you. It makes sense to you because your broker did his homework. Your intellect broker also makes a few commission dollars on your purchase. It may allow him to keep his desk on the floor for another month, instead of having it moved out to the parking garage.

Next, your broker calls his artist or musician clients. These clients could care less about why the Ripmobile 12 3/4 bonds are such a terrific deal. They may not even know what a "12 3/4" is. They're far more concerned about their next art show or concert.

The singer is recording a new album at three o'clock and is desperately working out kinks that the tenor sax has on track six of the backup. He gets the call.

"My broker? Okay, put him through. Jerry? What's up."

"Got a great idea here, looks like a slam dunk for a "double" in about six months. You wanna hear about it?"

"Yeah, but make it quick guy. I'm kinda' rushed."

"Well I've got this junk bond by a company that just came out with something really hot. The bond is at a heavy discount, but —."

"Jerry, you like it?"

"Yeah, I think it'll be real good for you."

"How much?"

"Put in about fifty, I'll watch it close."

"Fifty thousand? It's that good?"

"Yup, I —."

"Okay Jerry, keep me posted. Gotta go." Click.

Our singer friend is an astute investor. He just doesn't have the time to follow his investments. All he wants to know is that his broker is comfortable with the idea, and that he is comfortable with his broker.

There are two particularly unique opportunities available to all investment brokers. While these opportunities may be available to all brokers, the intellect truly recognizes and capitalizes on them.

The first opportunity is the ability to benefit from a diversity of knowledge. There may not be another occupation save perhaps politics, that demands such a broad base of knowledge, while constantly providing the resources to obtain it. An investment broker is deluged daily with vast amounts of information.

Political events directly affect investment decisions, as do ongoing social events. The broker is updated daily, hourly, and often on a moment by moment basis.

Constant exposure to various investment opportunities, acquaint him with specifics. What are the environmental concerns of the moment, and how is Tree-love Inc. responding to those concerns? Thirty minutes in a meeting about the latest hotel limited partnership will enlighten a broker as to how the boarding industry works, and what their concerns are. If he really follows the industry, the broker will be aware of issues like hotel security long before his favorite inn makes the television news magazine, over an increase in guest robberies.

Crime? Violence? How will it affect the rating on the municipal bonds of a given locality.

The intellect broker thrives on this opportunity to acquire diverse knowledge. He may not know everything about everything, but he probably knows more about most things than most people you will meet. It's his job.

The second opportunity that the investment broker has, is to benefit from life experiences. "So what," you say. "We all do." True, but probably not to the extent of the investment broker. The broker comes in contact with many different people from many different walks of life.

He constantly shares in the experiences of his or her clients. Our life experiences are multiplied by the number of social contacts we have. Your broker has many.

The intellect broker takes special delight in sharing with his clients, the wisdom he has gained from all of the various people he has dealt with. So does our next broker, the "investment consultant."

The Investment Consultant.

12

The Investment Consultant

One of the most difficult things for an investor to do is to determine what kind of broker he has. Don't try to accomplish this task by looking to the title of the person you are dealing with.

Today, almost everyone is called a "financial consultant" but almost no one knows exactly what a financial consultant is. The title has been brutally misused by brokerage companies, insurance companies and others in order to deceive the public as to who it is they are actually dealing with.

Your financial consultant may be an insurance person licensed only to provide insurance products. It may be a stock broker with anywhere from one day to three decades of investment experience. It might be a tax accountant, who took the Series 6 securities exam so he could supplement his income by selling you mutual funds as he prepares your tax return.

Many of these people are highly qualified to offer you expert financial advice and many more aren't. No formal license or regulation is required to use the title of financial consultant.

Webster's Seventh New Collegiate dictionary defines a consultant as "one who gives professional advice or services." It is also generally assumed that he is an expert in his chosen field. A financial consultant therefore, could be an expert in all things financial. Taxes. Investments. Law. Few investment brokers would fill this bill, but wait. The financial consultant could also be an expert in only one small segment of finance, say stock investing. The term is intentionally chosen for its vagueness.

To some, financial consulting might imply financial planning. In this chapter we want to look at the securities broker who integrates financial planning into his brokerage practice.

A financial planner looks at more than simply a given investment. He reviews your entire financial situation and attempts to establish a financial plan that will meet your objectives while maximizing your investment returns. His planning may be formal or informal. He may sit with you and write down your objectives, or he may simply learn over time what your needs and desires are. His knowledge of your financial requirements together with his knowledge of the different types of investments available, allow him to select only those investments that are best suited for you.

A financial planner may have a formal certification or he may not. A certified financial planner (CFP) has taken an extensive course in order to qualify for the designation. Among other things, the course includes studies in estate planning, insurance planning, tax planning, and investment planning.

A financial planner may charge a fee for his planning services, recommending that you go elsewhere to purchase the actual investments. This planner is called a "fee based" planner. The planner may be compensated only by commissions that he earns from the investments he places you in. This planner would be called a "commission based" planner. Some financial planners charge the fee and take the commissions too. This type of planner is called a lot of things—that we can't print in this book.

Some financial plans are general in nature. A general plan might simply suggest that you "open and IRA" (Investment Retirement Account) or "buy some Muni Bonds" (Tax free bonds). Other plans are far more specific. They recommend exactly which bonds, funds, or investments you should purchase. You might correctly assume that a commission based financial planner will be quite specific. He doesn't get paid until you actually purchase an investment. On the other hand, if you pay good money for ideas that still leave you searching for the actual investment vehicle, you might soon find yourself wishing your plan *had* been more specific. You still have to find (and pay for) the actual investment.

With all of these fancy terms and titles floating around, it's easy to get confused, so for the sake of clarity, I am going to take a liberty here. The stock broker who practices financial planning is a financial planner that works on commission. I am going to call him an "investment consultant."

The semantics are not important. What is important, is to recognizing who the person is and how he goes about his business. It may or may not be important if the investment consultant actually has a CFP designation. Many do, many others do not. While the CFP designation certainly can't hurt, a broker with prior legal or accounting experience, or one with related college degrees may very well satisfy you. It's the experience and the focus that matters.

The investment consultant is similar to the intellect except that he doesn't get quite as wrapped up in the details of an individual investment. His investment knowledge while extensive, is more general in nature. His focus is not so much that "this is a really great investment." Rather it's that "this is a really great investment *for this client.*" In order to make the last conclusion, it follows that the investment consultant has to know a lot about the client. "Knowing the client" is what financial planning and the investment consultant, are all about.

The successful investment consultant recognizes his weaknesses in other professional disciplines and will focus himself as one of three, of a client's financial advisors. He will happily work with, learn from and often educate the other two, the tax accountant and the lawyer. If the approach is successful, the client can truly boast of having a financial consulting team.

As with any relationship of two or more people, one single person will become the primary focus; the person relied on most often. This person will emerge as the director of your financial team. Your investment consultant will certainly strive to be this person. He will also be comfortable with the role. You probably talk to your tax accountant once a year, maybe twice. You chat with your attorney whenever you need him, hopefully not very much. You are on the phone with your investment consultant much more frequently if you have any kind of relationship at all, and by default, he will become your team leader unless you have a really strong or perhaps long term relationship with one of the other two.

In any case the investment consultant knows you, your circumstances and should be happy to conference with the other two players when needed. He should be comfortable talking with them. More importantly he should know when he has to. If you approach your broker (any broker) with a complicated question concerning your finances, and he refers you to one of your other team members, don't be disappointed with him. You should feel gratified. This broker knows when to tell you "I don't know the answer to that."

This three way consulting team can run into trouble at times. Sometimes the team players run into conflicts with each other.

The investment consultant and the lawyer will rarely have problems. The broker is not going to second guess the attorney very often. The broker doesn't practice law and will rarely if ever, question the attorney's advice unless he views it as blatantly wrong. Likewise, it is seldom that the attorney will offer investment advice to the client. It's not what he gets paid for.

The relationship between broker and accountant, however, can at times, create conflict.

Broker's often complain about accountants. There are usually three reasons for such complaints.

First reason. The accountant gave the client good advice making the broker look like a fool for not knowing the ramifications of his own advice. The broker had no idea what the client's situation really was, and the tax accountant faced with the choice of defending an unknown broker or protecting his client's interests, mysteriously chose the latter option. Ignorant broker. Good Accountant. The investment consultant goes way out of his way not to be ignorant about his client.

Second reason. The client really doesn't have an accountant. They only think they do. Instead they have a high school drop out who hung out a "Tax Service" shingle two months ago because he lost his day job. Rather than pay a reasonable fee to a proficient accountant, the client chose the "no load" service and got really bad advice. Basic, fundamental, "anyone who knows anything" *bad* advice. It can cost a client thousands of dollars very quickly. Even a novice broker knows the basic tax rules affecting investment decisions. You do have that tax section on the series 7 test. Good broker, lousy accountant.

Third reason. Good Accountant. Good Broker. Problem with accountant though. Thinks he's an investment advisor too. The good broker knows he's not an accountant. The good accountant knows he's no investment advisor. But some accountants seem to think they are investment advisors too. It can be trouble. Most good accountants would be hard pressed to jeopardize a great tax-client relationship with an investment recommendation that didn't work out. It's not their business.

Tax accountants that also make investment recommendations fall into three basic types.

The first type is the investment consultant that also practices tax accounting. This can be a very good person to deal with. If competent in both disciplines, this broker can serve as two of your three financial consultants. You have to understand, however, that he is using the tax service to supplement his commission business. The tax business brings in some extra money, but more importantly it brings in more investment clients. His focus is primarily on the commissions he makes from investments.

The remaining two accountants can be a real danger to both the investment consultant and the client.

The second type of accountant who offers investment advice, simply can't resist the urge to make a few extra commission dollars by recommending a mutual fund or two, to his tax clients. He'll usually pick something the wholesaler (the mutual fund representative) told him is "safe." He takes his fee for the tax return and then tacks on a commission, often five to ten times his tax service fee, by selling the fund. Your investment consultant probably knows that the fund you bought, just changed investment philosophy and can now put up to 40 percent of its money into junk bonds. The accountant was busy doing tax returns when news of the change came out.

The third type of accountant that provides investment advice, has more altruistic intentions. He looks at his clients, and feels he owes them some additional advice, along with the return. A "freebie" if you will. He feels it's his responsibility to save his clients from making investment mistakes. Being risk averse by nature, he simply tells them to go into one year T-Bills or CD's. "Nobody gets hurt in one year T-Bills. Stay safe. Go with one year T-Bills."

Two years later the retired couple desperately seeks the advice of the investment consultant. The T-Bills matured and at the new interest rate, the couple will take a 60% pay cut. At the new lower rate, they can't even afford to pay the rent any more. They are still raving about the great advice they got from their accountant but ask the broker, with anxious looks on their faces, "can you do any better?"

Remember the difference between those long and short term bonds? One preserves the principal and the other preserves the income? The investment broker knows this, but the accountant never gave it a thought.

The difference between the three brokers we have talked about so far, is simply this. The salesman is thinking about what might work so he can make a bigger commission. The intellect is thinking about the single best investment he or she knows of. Will the client benefit from my latest, and greatest idea? The investment consultant is trying to figure out what he can recommend, so the client can pay the rent again (or continue paying it). The investment consultant has a "quiver" of really solid investments to draw from. Which one of them will to allow his client to keep paying the bills?

Suffice it to say, the brokerage companies have caught on to the financial planning concept. Faced with the knowledge that their clients' real concern is food on the table and maybe a nice vacation or two, they have recognized the value of the investment consultant. One problem. They also know that the investment consultant and the intellect don't bring them as many commission dollars as their salesmen do. Faced with this knowledge and the understanding that many of their salesmen are too busy "cold calling" to spend the time it takes to develop a good financial plan, they have come up with a two part solution that they truly believe works for all.

First part? Simple. Rename the brokers! Simply call them all financial consultants or something similar.

Second part? Voila. Create the "canned financial plan." "What's a canned financial plan," you ask? It's a computer program that cranks out a financial plan. A form is filled out by the client (or his broker), listing everything financial there is to know about the client. It is then submitted to company headquarters and a group of certified financial planning graduates. These "specialists" mull over the information for a second or two, and then feed it in to a computer which prints out an instant financial plan. The plan is reviewed for a few minutes more, and is run through the legal and tax departments to make sure there are no really glaring errors. With its forty to seventy canned charts and graphs, it is then dumped back into the laps of the brokers, who are expected to spend two to four hours presenting the results of the masterpiece to their clients. For little or no compensation, of course. Most companies even charge for this service.

What could be better? A computerized, personalized financial plan done by people the client never even met or heard of, to take the place of the investment consultant's experience, ongoing advice, and knowledge. Now, the salesman can be an investment consultant too!

The company's have learned, in this process, something the investment consultant always knew. If they can learn everything there is to know about the client's finances, they are in a better position to make commissions off of those newly discovered assets. As a client though, you might want to consider whether there is a difference between divulging such private information to a single broker that you trust, versus divulging it to a company that can distribute it to any of its vast departments, for final use by a salesman who's primary concern is to make his next commission.

Some companies are so enthusiastic about their newest "financial planning" product, that they are literally *cramming it down the throats* of their brokers. The broker's are given a monthly quota, and are forced to do a certain number of plans each month. The canned financial plan is such a great deal the companies can't even *sell their own brokers*! They have to *force* their brokers to do them.

Serious investment consultants know full well that no individual's financial well being, can be so neatly packaged. They understand that investment consulting is not quite so easy. It's not so mathematical. Financial planning comes over time. It's all about really getting to know the client's needs, as they are and as they inevitably change. It's about knowing which investment options are available currently. Not yesterday, not tomorrow. The ones that will work for the client in the best possible way. It's about getting personal. It's knowing the accountant and the lawyer, at least on speaking terms. It's about being able to call the accountant and ask something as simple as if the estimated taxes have been filed yet, or as complicated as what the client's alternative minimum tax status is expected to be by the end of the year. It's knowing if the client's attorney put together the living trust yet, or where he stands on the new will.

The "financial consultant" doesn't exist, at least for most of us. Don't mistake a salesman for a financial consultant just because he offers you a financial plan that he's being forced to sell.

A financial plan that is done in conjunction with a competent broker, can be a very valuable tool. A financial plan that is done because it is forced on the broker, simply to uncover client assets so the broker can exploit them, is *not* a valuable tool. It is *dangerous to the client*. Period!

The "investment consultant", however, may very well be the most important person in your financial life. They just don't call him by his real name. You have to seek him out.

The Specialist.

13

The Specialist

Most if not all of the investment brokers we have talked about so far are generalists. That is to say they handle a variety of different investment products with more than a fair working knowledge of each. The Specialist is a different animal.

This is probably not your main broker. This is the guy you keep on the side, your second broker. He's a niche player, a true expert, but only in his chosen field of investments.

Let's get one thing straight right up front. There are specialists, and then there are brokers who pretend to be specialists. The broker we're discussing in this chapter is a true blue product specialist. It follows that, in order for a broker to be a product specialist, the product he deals in has to be complex enough to require a specialist in the first place.

Lots of broker's call themselves specialists. It sounds impressive and it makes for a great sales pitch.

"Good evening, Mr. Jones. My name is Henry and I specialize in tax free income. Do you think you might be paying too much taxes on your investment income? I specialize in how to save you taxes on your investment income."

Tax free investing is "Brokering 101." If someone calls you and happens to mention that he's a tax free specialist, hang up the phone. Any broker with more than a day of experience can buy a municipal bond or a derivative of same. If your broker isn't at the very least knowledgeable about tax free investing, get yourself another broker—and do it quickly.

Tax free investing is pretty straightforward. It really doesn't require a "specialist." You buy a bond, a fund or a trust, and once you get past the fundamentals of bonds there isn't much to it. There *are* true bond specialists, but they probably reside at company headquarters, in the bond trading department. They won't be calling you very often.

"I specialize in buying quality stocks for my clients."

Translation. "Whatever the company analyst has a buy on is a quality stock and I can look up those ratings real quick and put together a great stock portfolio for you."

"Okay," you might reply. "I have some certificates of Rathyon dated 1982. Can you tell me how much they're worth now? Did they split since then?"

"Sure, let me just look up the symbol for Rathyon."

Ah ha! You just asked a double trick question. Rathyon isn't exactly a super well known stock. But anyone who at least brokered through the Persian Gulf War will probably know RTN is the symbol for the company that manufactures the Patriot Missile. If your broker is busy looking up the symbol, it's a real good bet that he hasn't been around long — especially long enough to be your specialist. Part two of the trick question. So the stock split. If it did, they sent you the extra shares. "Just tell me how many shares you have. I'll punch up RTN on the old quote machine and have your value for you inside of, lets say thirty seconds."

There are a lot of make believe product specialists out there, ready to dazzle you blind with how much they don't know. The tax specialist. The stock specialist. And yes, the Trader. Ask your alleged trading specialist how the moving average convergence divergence indicator looked on your favorite stock yesterday. While you're at it ask him where the stochastics are and if it's consolidating within the Bollinger bands. These are all highly complex trading signals that a good trader will be able to call up on his computer almost instantly. You'll weed out a lot of "trading specialists" by asking how the charts look on their computers. You don't have to know what these signals mean, but if your trading specialist doesn't, you've got a problem.

There's another kind of so called specialist that deserves some attention here, the "client specialist."

This is the broker that claims to specialize in a certain type of client. Almost by definition a client specialist is a product generalist, because almost all kinds of clients need exposure to a general variety of investments. But there are certain categories of clients that possess a majority of investable funds these days. "Specialists" have, of course, cropped up to handle their needs. Are you one of these clients?

"Gee, Mr. Jones, sorry to hear about the recent loss of your job. How long did you say you were with the company?"

"Eighteen years."

"Sir, I'm really glad I caught you tonight. I just happen to be a specialist in retirement distributions and rollovers. Did you have a pension or 401K that you now have to make a decision on?"

How about this one?

"How long did you say you're retired? I specialize in *"conservative"* investment plans for retired people. How much did you say you have in CD's? We really should talk."

There may be a *slight* area of specialization in these two circumstances. It may be that your broker has a lot of experience with other clients who had the misfortune to get "excessed" from the same company. He knows the specifics of their retirement plan and how to get it transferred into an account that you and he can control. Dealing with retired people can take more than the average amount of understanding, depending on the client. But if you're retired your investment situation is still not so different from many others. A good broker understands his or her client, be they fired, retired or happily employed earning seven hundred thousand a year. The individual may be different, but the investment concepts are the same. We're all in the same markets.

So who then is the real specialist—this guy you keep in your hip pocket for when you need him? He's the broker that is really good at a specific product. If you want to put a few bucks into his specific area of expertise, no one else will do. No one else knows more about it. A few examples come to mind.

Real Estate Limited Partnerships. You will remember that this is where you pool your money with others, going partners to buy real estate. These are investments that you really can't sell very easily if you want to. A lot of people have had bad experiences with these investments. Usually it's because they bought them from someone other than a specialist who really knew how to tell the good from the bad. This is a product that requires very "in depth" understanding. Limited partnerships don't trade on the exchanges. You can't determine their value from a quote in the paper. There's not a whole lot of information published about them—it's mostly the quarterly reports and such. You have to study them. You have to spend time on them. You have to really love them. You have to have the contacts to buy and sell them. You have to have a whole lot of knowledge about them, in order not to get burned.

A real good stock specialist is hard to find. This isn't the broker who simply has a passing fancy in some stock that the company analyst is raving about. This is the broker who really does his homework. He studies the company, perhaps even calling them—often. He does his fundamental work ups. He knows all of the pertinent information off the top of his head. He knows what industry the company operates in, and whether or not it's the industry of choice in the current investment climate. He knows how the company ranks in its industry, its share of market, new product lines, its management, the works. This broker probably wouldn't buy you a mutual stock fund if his office depended on it. It's a matter of pride. He's a pro and you can buy some really superior stocks based on his dedication and research.

A new Specialist making the rounds over the last few years is the "Wrap Fee broker." For those of you who are not familiar with this product I'll expand for a moment.

This is a program where you bring your $100,000 plus to a broker. He interviews you to determine your individual tolerance for investment risk. You and he fill out and sign off on ten to fifteen forms full of tiny legal print. Based on your answers to the questions on the forms, the broker guides you in the selection of a "money manager." The money manager is the professional that will actually be investing your money on a discretionary basis (meaning he doesn't have to call you to make investment changes). The wrap program includes finding the right manager for you, all of your trading commissions, the brokerage account service and a very fancy analysis every quarter or so, that your broker goes over with you. It explains how well, or not so well, the money manager has done for you. You go about doing what ever it is you do for a living and don't worry about it until the quarterly review. For all of these services you pay a fee of about three percent of your invested assets each year. The fee drops as greater amounts are invested.

Out of your three percent the money manager usually gets one percent. This, by the way, is the guy doing the work. The other two percent goes to the brokerage company and the broker gets his grid payout, let's say thirty two percent. For as long as you're in the program you keep paying. For as long as you're in the program, your broker keeps getting paid. Thirty two percent of two percent? About sixty four, one hundredths, of a percent. Not much you say, but it builds. On ten million bucks, it's sixty four thousand. It's a living. It's a better living on twenty or thirty million and for a good wrap fee specialist such numbers are realistic. But he has to work at it. He has to study the money managers. He has to go over those quarterly reports with each of those clients at least the first couple of times. It's often very time consuming trying to keep clients in the program, after they've seen the performance their three percent has actually bought them.

A lot of brokers try to do "wrap" business. A lot more would like to. How else can a broker build an annuity in commissions from often mediocre performance? Despite my personal distaste for this product (everyone's entitled to an opinion even if it's only a professional one), it is a specialty.

There are other specialties. Brokers are individuals, with different likes and dislikes, as are we all. They will eventually prefer areas of investing which are most to their liking. It might be trading stocks (short term investing for maximum gain). It might be convertible preferred stocks and bonds (issues that convert into common stock at certain times). These investments do take research above and beyond the norm. It might also be mutual funds. We discussed mutual funds in chapter two, but lets talk about them some more.

A mutual fund can be purchased just about anywhere these days. Brokerage companies have them, banks now have them and of course you can go direct to the fund. You can also buy mutual funds to invest in just about anything you could ever want to invest in. There are tax free funds, taxable bond funds, junk bond funds, equity funds which could invest in growth stocks, value stocks, dividend stocks, and or small to mid-cap stocks. You could buy a fund that goes global or foreign, in stocks or bonds or both. You could probably buy a fund that only invests in politically correct, socially conscious, mid-cap stocks in lower California that are no more that five but no less than three years old and have growth estimated to be greater than thirty five percent in each of the next fourteen quarters.

You can buy proprietary funds (those run by brokerage houses and sometimes banks), independent funds, no-load funds and load funds, A shares, B shares and now the recent C shares. Oh yes, you can also buy open or closed funds. With such a limited selection, why in the world would someone think they need a mutual fund specialist. Especially with all of those financial magazines telling us which funds are having their momentary "day in the sun."

What is the difference between the broker generalist who will put you into a fund, and the specialist who will put you into a *good* fund?

It's lunch time. The local fund wholesaler for XYX mutual fund is in to buy the brokers lunch and tell them all about his great new fund (it may be an older fund that happens to be having a good year). The fund wholesaler is an employee of the fund. It's his or her job to sell the fund to the brokers, and through them, to you. Let's not ignore the importance of this person. The wholesaler is the main contact between the broker and the fund. This person has lunch with the people that actually run the funds. The wholesaler can provide valuable information as to the current thinking or philosophy of the fund manager. A good wholesaler is invaluable to your broker.

But if you think you're a tough sell, you haven't seen anything until you've seen someone try to sell your broker. Courtesy abounds at these meetings but your broker, specialist or not, has seen it all. The wholesaler has to be really good to set his fund apart from countless others. How does he or she do this?

There's the obvious. Higher payout, trailers (that's when the broker continues to get paid after the fund is sold), maybe a special commission promotion for the next three weeks. There are other ways to get the job done. Cute little T-shirts with the fund's name on them, that the broker can wear to the beach, while doing his gardening, or perhaps give to his wife to wear as a night shirt. Golf trips are nice. "Put only $250,000 in my fund by the end of the month and we'll all go out to the nineteenth hole, courtesy of the fund." If your broker has just been offered a trip to Hawaii for putting only a million or so of his client's money into a certain fund, you had better be sure he has your best interests in mind, not hula skirts, when your phone rings.

The most obnoxious of all fund wholesalers, is the company representative for the proprietary products of the brokerage firm, if the firm has them. This fellow has, by virtue of his management position in the brokerage company, a captive audience. He's probably somebody's son, because on his own merits he wouldn't be able to get a job as a dog catcher. After taking up an extra hour and a half of the broker's valuable time touting the boring attributes of his product, he sets himself apart from the rest of the wholesalers very simply. "Do this fund or lose your job." Okay, so maybe I paraphrased him a tiny little bit, but the very real threat to your broker, is there.

There are other things that will of course, set a fund apart, and *these are the things* that your fund specialist is looking for. Performance is nice. A particularly unique investment approach or philosophy by the fund manager can be real interesting. An unusual niche that would fit nicely into client portfolios, complimenting their current investments? Always interesting.

The specialist will check the fund's numbers against an independent source or two, to see if all the things he normally looks for, the characteristics he wants, are there. He has probably even spent some of his own money to access this information. He cares. He wants to know what the real track record is. What's the risk? The specialist is not going to present a fund to anyone, until he's sure he would buy it himself. In fact, he may even buy it himself and hold it for a couple of months to see how it's doing.

Let's not get confused about all of this specialty stuff. If you go to your specialist looking for something he doesn't specialize in, he's not going to turn you down. Few brokers will suggest you take your business elsewhere if you don't want to buy their specialty. You just have to understand that, at this point, you are dealing with a generalist. You'll probably get the "house special." The specialist probably doesn't do the same research on another type of investment that he does on his specialty. He doesn't have the interest.

There's another thing you should understand when dealing with the specialist. He knows his *investment area* very well, but he may not *know you* so very well. This broker is not often the "investment consultant." As a client, you may want to take special care to insure that the investment he specializes in, *is correct for you.* The specialist is extremely prejudice and may often place people in his investments, that really don't belong there.

You will know pretty quickly if you have a broker that is a specialist. You can tell very easily by the types of products he consistently presents to you. By nature he will prefer, and present his strength. This certainly isn't a bad thing. After all, you wouldn't want him offering you investments he knows little or nothing about, would you?

Lets move on to our final two brokers. One is a real good guy, the other isn't. Both of them can *really cost you money.*

Two more Broker Types.

14

Two More Broker Types

So far we have discussed a number of different styles of brokering. They range from brokers that you would want to bank your last buck with to brokers that you will be okay with. While their styles may differ considerably, if you have one of the brokers we have already discussed, you'll probably survive. You may in fact, do very well.

Now we're going to touch on a couple of brokers that can seriously hurt you. These two different brokers couldn't be more diametrically opposed. One is honest, sincere and above board in all of his dealings. The other couldn't give a good "gosh darn" about you.

The first of these brokers will be most difficult to part company with. You may have dealt with him or her for years. The other you should have no problem losing in an instant.

They are the "semi-retired broker" and of course, the "out and out fraud."

Let's talk about the semi-retired broker first. In the brokerage business it is all too easy to lay back, once you've got a substantial book of business.

After fifteen to twenty years, a broker's book will support him. There is always enough business in his client base to allow him a decent living. With any luck at all that business keeps referring other new clients that continue to bring in commission dollars. The problem is, that with fifteen years or more in the brokerage business, one can really burn out.

Lets clarify what we're talking about here. We are *not* talking about the five or eight year broker who just can't take it any more. We're not talking about "foot loose Charlie" who has a good business and likes to take a lot of time off to go golfing, meet new people, and raise new money.

We're talking about the broker with *lots* of years in the business. His total "book" (assets under management) can easily run up over fifty million. He has lots of experience. Lots of long term relationships. Lots of income. But to him, the whole thing is getting very tiring.

By default, this broker is very good at his trade. If he wasn't he wouldn't have lasted all these years. He wouldn't have fifty million plus, very happy dollars under management. He wouldn't have survived the stock brokerage business for that amount of time, without being very good at what he does. He also has to have a large number of very happy long term clients, probably also mostly retired by now.

He starts thinking.

"Whether I sit around the office or not, I'm worth about two hundred big ones a year, because those commission dollars will keep rolling in. I don't need to be in the office every hour the markets are open. I can call a few clients when I get around to it and make all of the money I need to. Hmmm. I can go golfing anytime or anywhere I want. The bucks will still come rolling in. Maybe I should back down to two or three days a week. I could spend my leisure time golfing and put more time into my new hobbies, basket weaving and clay sculptures. Who would care.

"I'll call a few clients on the days I'm in and update them on the markets. The company's not going to exactly kick me out—not with seven fifty in annual production. If they try to, I'll tell them to take a flying leap. Besides, I really owe myself and my spouse a few more vacations during the year. For all the ones I missed when I was building my "book."

The broker starts to ease off. As his client you can tell very easily. Four out of five times you call him he's "out on appointment." "He'll get back to you tomorrow, or in a day or two, or maybe a week or two."

"Gee, I really need to speak to someone. My IBM's falling like a rock. Is there someone I could talk to?"

"S-u-u-r-e." The broker's backup, or perhaps the broker of the day. There's not a broker in the office that won't be happy to talk to you. They all know your guy is not going to be around too much longer and if they can establish an ongoing relationship with you, who are you going to ask for when he retires?

Before you know it you have an ongoing relationship with about five different brokers in the office. Once every two or three months your real broker calls to say hello. You feel relieved. "Charlie's back."

Now you've got to understand something here. The other brokers in Charlie's office love to chat with you when they have the time, but they *don't get paid for it.* Charlie still gets all the commissions. If one of these guys handles a trade for you, you're still Charlie's client and it's still Charlie that gets paid. It's a courtesy thing.

Two things are happening here, both of which you are probably unaware. First, your account is not getting reviewed on a regular basis. It's the weekly or biweekly reviews that can spot problems in your account before they become a crisis. Picture ole' Charlie kicking back on the beach in Acapulco with his portable computer, going over your account while ordering three "Sex on the Beach's" and yacking it up with five couples that he just made friends with (they're prospects, actually). "Yeah, right."

Then the second thing happens. You wake up one Wednesday morning and as you recover from your deep sleep, your clock alarm radio is chanting on and on about how they just dropped the nuke in Korea, the president just resigned over his thirty fifth tax evasion disclosure, Sadamm is back in town blowing up Kuwait oil fields, the Resolution Trust just declared bankruptcy and with it, the Federal Deposit Insurance Company just announced that it is no longer going to insure any CD's over twenty cents because five of the largest banks in the country just defaulted on their bond payments—because twenty three third world countries have decided not to pay their loans for the next ten or twenty decades.

This news dwarfs itself however, to the one liner that is given to Hopscotch, your biggest holding. Something about their Chief Executive Officer being arrested and hauled off in handcuffs at one o'clock in the morning for insider trading or something.

As you drive to work the radio dwells on all of the events of the day but fails to mention anything more about good old "Hopscotch." The sweat begins to roll off of your forehead and the steering wheel gets slippery under the palms of your hands—so slippery in fact that as you turn to avoid the pretty young thing in the Camaro that just cut you off, your steering wheel slips and you nail her in the left rear quarter panel.

You arrive in your office, bruised but not beaten. The markets are down two fifty and you figure you better give old Charlie a call to see if he can make it all better.

"Sorry, He's out on appointment." Yeah, you mutter under your breath. In Honolulu, with three more sombrero's. You respond just as you have been for the last six months.

"Is there someone else that could help me?"

"I'll try to have someone get back to you sir. It's kind of busy here today." You picture the office. Broker's jumping up and down, yelling into phones at the top of their lungs. "Well how 'bout Harry? I spoke with him last week. Is he in?"

"Yes sir, I'll tell him, but he's on the phone right now and has six calls waiting." Yup. Harry has his own clients, and they pay him.

"Uh, good, I'll wait." and your phone starts playing Beethoven's "- Andante in F". As you listen to the pretty music, your mind starts running wild. You think lots of thoughts but the one thought you don't think about because you don't realize it, is that Harry is not going to give you a recommendation. Nope. Unwritten rule between brokers. Never make a recommendation to another broker's client. In fact, as much as he likes you, Harry really doesn't have much time to give you right now. In fact Harry really doesn't want to talk to you at all right now.

Eight calls later, (Harry took two more of his client's calls before he picked you up) you breath a sigh of relief.

"Mr. Smith, hi, it's Harry. Sorry to keep you waiting, it's kind of hectic here today."

You're being rushed. You can tell.

"Uh, Hi, Harry. I'll just take a minute. I heard the CEO of Hopscotch got arrested today. How's the stock?"

"Hopscotch? Uhm. Let me check the symbol." Minutes of raw panic pass. Harry comes back.

"Yup, it's down five points. It gapped down four and headed on south. Yup, got the news now. They got him on inside information. You wanna' sell?"

"Gee, I don't know. Five points on a twenty dollar stock, do you think I should?"

You get the classic "I don't want to make a recommendation to another broker's client" response.

156 —

"Well, I don't follow this one sir. I can't make a recommendation. Oops. Can you hold a minute, got another call I've gotta take."

"Yeah, I'll hold."

After what seemed like a two year hold, you decided to sell Hopscotch. All five thousand shares. Harry didn't know the stock. He took your sell order and got you fourteen and three eighths. Harry didn't notice that, two days ago Hopscotch reported earnings increases of fifty three percent. He also wasn't aware that the CEO they nailed was hated by everybody on the street, and that his second in command (the new CEO) is one of the most capable managers in the "Scotch" industry. Four hours later the stock recovered and it closed the day at twenty two bucks. Flat, even though the markets tanked for the day.

Charlie didn't know about it either but the Hula girls were great. Hey. He's in ten year bonds now!

You go home for the day. As you're sipping your third Martini the phone rings.

"Good evening Mr. Smith. My name is Gerald. Have I got a hot stock for you!"

"Who's Gerald?" you mumble to yourself angrily. You should know the answer. Gerald is your "out and out fraud." He goes on.

"This baby's priced at twenty five cents and it's gonna go to heaven by the end of the week. Take ten thousand shares and you won't be sorry." Gerald is never low key.

You think to yourself, "O - kay. After today, what's another twenty five hundred bucks? Maybe I'll get lucky and make back Hopscotch."

"Okay, I'll bite. What da ya need, my social security number?"

Gerald did have a problem. He got lucky though. You just solved it for him. His company's been trading this worthless stock all the way up from three cents, which incidentally, was where he got his father to buy it. Now his father wants *out*, and the company has no market for the dog. Until he got you. It's a "penny stock." The brokerage company makes the market and the market is what ever they can get for a hot story with no numbers behind it.

It's called "trading the book." The stock is traded from one client to the next, until the bubble bursts.

Actually Gerald got very lucky. Usually he has to "prep" his prospects for a month or so with maybe three or four calls, before they'll buy. It doesn't matter to Gerald. He makes forty thousand a month in a good month. When the bubble bursts, his company closes up shop and opens up another brokerage company under another name and/or license. When Gerald burns out he gets another job or puts his bucks in bonds, and lives happily off the interest.

You'd be amazed how easy it is to get people to part with two or three thousand dollars for a lousy stock, if it's hyped right. You'd be equally amazed how hard it is to get the same people to part with fifty or a hundred thousand, for a solid blue chip mutual fund, or a tax free bond or two. Gerald's on the phone fifteen hours in any given day but the commissions on those two thousand dollar bills really add up.

Be *real careful*, if you happen to have one of these two brokers.

There may be good and bad stock brokers, but no industry could survive for as long, and make so much money as this one has, without adding some serious value to the investment process. Those of you who have a good broker know that. Perhaps those of you who disagree, simply haven't found a good broker yet, or perhaps you haven't been a very good client.

Now we're going to talk about the one thing in the broker-client relationship that can really damage the investment returns. *The client!*

Clients usually break down into three categories. Good, Bad and Great, but make no mistake about it. Nothing can ruin a client's portfolio like a client.

Knowing what kind of client you are, and how you rank on your broker's priority list, can be very helpful. Knowing what other kinds of clients your broker deals with, may make you a *better* client. And it just might make you *a lot more money*.

The Good Client.

15

The "Good" Client

There's a time-honored rule in the investment brokerage industry: Eighty percent of the business comes from twenty percent of the clients.

The great client is worth the eighty percent. The bad client is worth little or nothing. This chapter covers the twenty percent, the "Good" clients. They are not going to make or break the broker, but they always do nice business. They are almost always nice people and they are often fun to work with. Besides, it may be twenty percent of the business, but it's still eighty percent of the book. Who in their right mind would turn away twenty percent of their annual income?

Let's start with the "Quiet/Good" client. This client always feels like he's bothering you. The broker usually wishes this client would bother him just a little more. This client has every attribute of a great client, save one. He really doesn't do much business. He's probably got money. Maybe not a lot, but at the very least he's comfortable. He makes fast decisions. He may labor for hours at home deciding what he wants to do, but when he calls his broker, he's ready. He's smart. He's savvy. He's usually conservative. He can afford to be. He has enough money to be able to take the most conservative approach to investing and still live very nicely off of it.

If the broker calls him with an idea or a thought, this client knows in an instant whether it will work for him or not. He lets the broker know it too. More often it will not, but he always appreciates the call. If the broker has an idea or two that strike him, it's a done deal. It's simple. Every so often he'll give his broker a call with an extra twenty or forty thousand that he's looking to place.

He has one broker. Nobody else. Together they have done well over the years, and when this client needs to spend some money in the markets, the broker is his first and only call. Does the broker make a whole lot of money off of this client? Nope, but when he does, it's a pleasure.

The next good client is the "analyst." The analyst is probably a professional in one of the more exacting practices, such as accounting or engineering. He is trained in a precise world, to eliminate even the remotest chance of risk or error.

Markets, especially financial markets, are subjective, intuitive. The analyst is objective and methodical. Analysts are almost always very smart people, but everything in their world has to add up precisely, or it simply doesn't work. The analyst just doesn't understand that investing isn't always a mathematical science. It's more of an art.

The analyst calls his broker on the telephone with his latest idea. Everything he says about it makes sense. Analytically it's a "no lose". He may even spend countless time selling the broker on his idea. Rationally it's perfect, but somewhere in the depths of her broker's mind the broker knows the idea won't work. If it does, it will take the rest of the market forever to catch up with the brilliance of the analyst's thinking. The selling process starts to work in reverse. The broker is not selling the client anymore. The client is selling the broker. The broker gives in and agrees with him. She buys the investment for the client. She won't touch it herself even though she's beginning to want to. It sounds great, but it just doesn't feel right and the broker has been burned far to many times by things that don't feel right.

Of course the investment takes a dive nine times out of ten. The broker loves the analyst. He's sharp and clever, not to mention the fact that he has a few bucks to spend. She groans when the analyst's latest, greatest idea drops in value. Not to worry though. The analyst will never sell. His investment *will* eventually be discovered. It may be a year. It may be longer, but this client's wisdom and analytical expertise will eventually be rewarded. The broker wins too. She watches the investment like a hawk. When it does start to get noticed by the rest of the market, the broker jumps on it in a flash.

If the broker calls the analyst with an absolute "must do now at all costs to preserve capital" recommendation, the analyst probably won't do it. He will wait until he's had the chance to think it over. By then we all know it's going to be to late.

An analyst really works well with an intellectual broker. He needs a broker that can work with him into the night and on into the next week using facts, figures and statistics to determine whether the idea is a good or bad one. Then the intellect broker can debate him on into the next decade using similar rational as to why her idea is better. Unfortunately the analyst doesn't often accept an intellect broker. He often prefers a younger broker with no distinctly developed traits. It allows the analyst to maintain his intellectual superiority. The young, inexperienced broker will be his "easy sell," and regardless of how the investment works out the analyst will feel good about it. The young broker will "yes" him to death.

The "get rich quick" client is interesting. A lot of brokers won't deal with him. Others do. They try to turn him into a trader. If they are successful and can keep him from blowing himself up, he gets to be an good client. Often even a great client.

The get rich quick has only one objective. He wants to make money in the markets, and he wants to make it fast. At first, his demands are outrageous but if the broker can work with him and bring him down to a level of reality, this client can make money. After a while the get rich quick learns the risks of a fast market and the equivalent risks of fast trading.

The get rich quick gets frustrated very quickly. He also gets gratified very quickly. If he's down he's upset. If he's up he's in heaven. The trick in dealing with a get rich quick is to calm him down.

Another very interesting thing about some get rich quick clients is that they only want to get rich quick with a small amount of their liquid funds. The rest of their money is often held in liquid investments (Money markets, CD's or the like). Once they realize their broker has more to offer than a few fast trades, the client starts approaching the broker with questions about the serious money. With the serious money, the get rich quick can be a really good client.

The "Nibbler" is also interesting. The nibbler is most comfortable buying only small amounts of investments. Before long, her four hundred thousand dollar account is filled with countless two to five thousand dollar holdings which become almost impossible to control. She is seriously "over diversified." Her account goes nowhere because, no matter how good the investment is, she doesn't own enough of it to make a difference. The broker can't afford to monitor all of these little holdings very closely. It usually doesn't matter. The nibbler rarely sells a poor investment. The nibbler is elated when one of her investments rises by fifty percent, but she fails to notice that its affect on her total portfolio, is *meaningless*!

The final good client is "Thrifty." Thrifty thinks the broker works for the fun of it. This client comes from all walks of life and a good broker can deal with all of them. It's not always pleasant but he can do it. He has to constantly argue the value of both his services and those of the investments he selects. Often, Thrifty refuses great investments because of the commission cost. Occasionally he'll submit and pay.

Thrifty is usually a nice person, but he hasn't learned yet, that investment products are like anything else. You get what you pay for. After these clients have been "penny wise and pound foolish" a few times, they usually begin to learn. Then they become really good clients. If they don't learn they simply make less money, and lose what they have faster that other clients who are willing to pay for value. Thrifty definitely doesn't get the broker's first calls. The broker may really like Thrifty on a personal level, but if a great idea comes up and the broker needs yes or no answers in a hurry, he simply can't afford to call Thrifty first. He can't spend valuable time arguing commissions, or negotiating yet another discount, when he has plenty of clients that are ready to act on value—and pay for it. It wouldn't be fair to the broker's *paying* clients, if he didn't offer them his ideas first, and review their accounts in far greater detail.

Good clients usually do well with their investments but they have three basic flaws that can really cost them money at times. First, they allow commissions to dictate their investments. They really dislike paying for value. Because of this, they often miss out on great opportunities. Their second flaw is that they usually hate to sell an investment, especially if it's losing money. Perhaps again, this is because they don't want to pay the commission cost of selling. The final basic flaw with the good client, is indecision. Many good clients have a difficult time making investment decisions. Their broker makes suggestions to them, but by the time they decide what to do they have usually lost money.

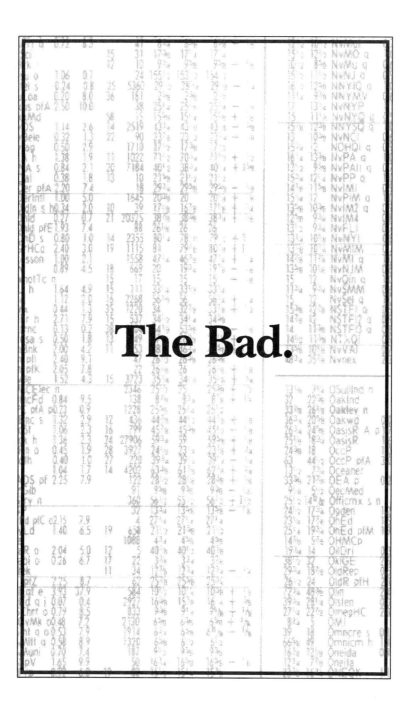

The Bad.

16

The Bad

If you've been through a lot of different brokers and are still dissatisfied maybe there's a reason. It may be because you have single-handedly suffered worse luck in finding a broker, than any of several million other people. That's possible, but highly unlikely.

More likely, is the fact that you are truly a bad client and all of your previous brokers have fired you.

You've got to understand something here. When a broker fires a client, he doesn't call him at 4:00 on a Friday afternoon and casually mention that the client is fired. On very rare occasions, though, a broker may simply tell a client that he really doesn't wish to work for them any more.

"Please find another broker because I am simply not going to handle your account any more."

Does this sound harsh? Perhaps, but there are clients that are so difficult to work with, and that have already been fired by so many brokers, they will refuse to give up on their broker until he flat out tells them it's over. They keep looking for new brokers (often brokers new to the business) and having found one, refuse to give him up no matter how badly they get treated. In fact, these clients refuse most everything. The biggest thing they refuse to do is to try to become a good or at least an okay client. It's simply not in their blood.

Most bad clients don't get the flat out "I'm not going to deal with you" treatment. They're fired in different ways. It is not in a broker's best interest to blatantly alienate anyone.

When a broker fires a client he usually does it in a more subtle way. He gradually takes the client off of his mailing list. He only returns calls after the markets close, or perhaps on the next day. The broker gives this client vague answers to his questions (the client really doesn't want to know what the broker thinks any way). The broker doesn't call this client with real potential winners. Why should he? The client rarely if ever buys anything. Eventually, the client finds another broker and without so much as a call the old broker gets a "transfer" (a report that another company has assumed the account and the account will be transferred out to them).

"Thank you God," the broker whispers to himself.

It's not personality that makes a bad client.

There are very good clients who are pleasant to deal with, always say hello to the staff, and are genuinely pleasing personalities. These are fun people to deal with.

There are also very good clients that are obnoxious. They are rude, abrupt, insulting to the staff and seem to take absolute delight in being nasty to people. If it makes them feel good to know that every one they meet quickly learns to hate them as a person, so be it. They pay commissions.

Personalities aside however, there are really bad client traits. Lets talk about a few.

First, there is KNOW-IT-ALL.
There are actually two types of know-it-all. The first one thinks he knows everything there is to know about invest-

ing. In fact he knows so much about everything that he's more than willing to spend two or three hours trying to convince the broker that his latest worthless investment idea is going to make millions for him, the broker and everyone else that knows about it. If the broker even thinks about disagreeing with the know-it-all, another two to four hours will go by debating why the know-it-all is right and the broker is wrong, about the client's super idea on how to make a million on "ABC junk stock" in thirty days or less. The broker can't win with this client. He tries though.

"If you like it so much, why don't you buy it."

"Well—. I want to watch it for a few days (the know-it-all means years.) Tell ya what, keep an eye on it for me and let me know when it's ready to buy, okay?"

"It's as ready to buy now as it'll ever be. I don't think it'll ever go any higher."

"Great. Buy it!" So the know-it-all breaks down and buys fifty shares.

Bottom line? This client will call the broker three times a day to discuss "Junk Stock." He'll even suggest how many "other brokers" love his stock. Right, the brokers that are more than anxious to take his money than concern themselves over whether or not their client loses money. The know-it-all never buys *enough* of the stock to make any money, even if it *did* go up. He just likes to fantasize about all the money he *would* make if he had bought it. He continues to hope that the stock will go up for a few days so he can say "I told you so."

The second know-it-all never actually becomes a client. He admittedly starts out knowing nothing, but all is not lost. He decides to learn everything there is to know about investing—in thirty days or less. Usually this person has come into some money rather rapidly. It could be a few thousand dollars or it could be much more.

This is a know-it-all in training. He begins his education by subscribing to about twenty newsletters and five or ten financial magazines. He then commences his "learning process" in earnest. He calls ten to fifty different brokers to get an idea of how they would handle his new-found wealth.

A broker can recognize one of these people in a fifth of an instant. He picks up the phone and all of a sudden he's being interviewed. This person has probably never interviewed anyone in his entire life, so he's not really very good at it.

"If I gave you my twenty-two thousand, four hundred and fifty dollars what exactly would you invest it in today so that it would become four hundred ninety eight thousand, six hundred fifty two dollars and ninety six cents, by this time next year? Oh, by the way, what would the annualized return on that be, anyway?"

Okay, so I'm exaggerating a little. Not very much, though. The funny part, is that they're dead serious when they ask their questions. The know-it-all in training will take hours of the broker's time, trying to learn in a few short days, what it took the broker years to learn.

This person never actually becomes a client. The month that he has allowed himself to "learn the business" becomes a year, then two—then many. Perhaps he takes a quick stab at a stock or fund rated A #1 for the last six months and gets cooked for a couple of thousand during the following six months.

Rather than make such a silly mistake again, he makes the biggest mistake of all. He *never* invests again. He never hires a broker. He continues his "educational search" for years. While everyone else is making money, the know-it-all in training gratifies himself by doing "what if analysis" over the last five years. He wants to test his financial acumen to see if it has reached the point where he can safely put his real money to work.

The WANNA BE BROKER is a person any broker will try to avoid. They come in various forms but they generally have a couple of things in common. They think investing is a fun game, like the slots. They rarely buy anything, often because they have no money. Wanna be brokers have no idea what the business is all about. They think the broker does nothing but sit around watching the stock tape all day. At 11:00 the broker calls fifty clients about a hot stock and by 3:45 he sells everybody out at a two hundred percent profit. Such a job!

The wanna be can be similar to the know-it-all, but he takes it a step or two further. He has no problem making countless "appointments" so he can "discuss the markets." He may not even bother to make an appointment. His broker is only sitting around waiting to talk to him anyway. He'll just "drop by." When he has decided what not to buy, he sits at the broker's desk for a couple of hours watching his only holding, two thousand dollars of worthless stock, trade the tape.

"Oh, go ahead with what you have to do. I'll just sit here and watch for awhile."

The broker really needs this guy at his desk when he has to call another client about a strategy on a four hundred thousand dollar portfolio.

"Excuse me, but I have to make a confidential call now."

"Gee, Bing Bang Boom is up another sixteenth. Do you think it will hit twenty soon?"

The stock is at $2.00 and is going bankrupt. Why should it hit twenty any time during the decade?

"I've really got to get back to work now, have a nice day." The broker stands up, the universal "body language" signal that the meeting is over. Wanna be doesn't speak "body language."

"It's okay, I'll just sit here and watch."

It's a casino game to the wanna be. When he goes to Vegas he can stand around the poker table all day and no one will kick him out unless he betrays a hand.

When the broker finally forces him out of the office, he calls four more times during the afternoon to see if his Bing Bang Boom hit twenty yet. After all, he owns a hundred shares and "isn't that what he pays the broker for?" Actually, he never paid the broker anything. He probably bought the shares somewhere else and had them transferred in.

Why does a broker put up with the wanna be, or any other bad client, to begin with? Usually because the client dangles a carrot in front of him. The client doesn't have any money but a relative or spouse might. The relative or spouse learned long ago not to trust their lucky bucks to this guy but for a time he makes the broker believe that he can influence those bucks in the broker's direction. Eventually the broker comes to realize that there's no percentage in the relationship and he fires the wanna be.

The BUDDY is another fun fellow. The buddy wants to be the broker's partner, but unlike a true partner, the buddy has nothing at all to contribute to the relationship. All of a sudden this perfect stranger who first bought fifty shares of a two dollar stock, has all of these great ideas for his broker. The only problem is that he has no serious money. This client too, will spend a lot of the broker's time trying to convince him how great his ideas are.

"Lets go to lunch." The broker of course should pay. "I'd like to share some super investment ideas with you.

Maybe we could go partner." Right. Crummy idea, not worth the price of the napkin it's sketched on and he wants the broker to put up the money for it.

"Love to meet you and the family. Why don't you and the lady come over for a barbecue next weekend? We've got a lot in common. By the way, could you bring a six pack?" The broker thinks back to the last afternoon he spent at a buddy's barbecue: burned hamburgers and burned french fries in a two by nothing back yard with un-mowed grass and no pool or a green pool. The "lady" got sick. She would have been okay, the broker thinks to himself, if she had been able to drink the Michalob he brought, but that went right into fridge only to be replaced with belch beer that was yellow before the cap was even popped. Yup. The broker does have quite a bit in common with this client. They both live on the same planet!

After a moment of reflection, the broker replies instinctively, "Gee, no. I'm really sorry but I have an appointment with my dentist for root canal and I just can't pass it up. Love to take a rain check though, sometime in my next life perhaps."

The overwhelming trait of a really bad client is that he or she takes an inordinate amount of the broker's time and does precious little business to pay for it. A second trait is that they often think they own the broker. Brokers are a very independent lot. You have to have a lot of money and be a really great client, to own a broker.

If you are a really bad client, you can rest assured your broker will desperately try to find a way to fire you.

The Great.

17

The Great Clients

There are lots of really good clients. Most clients are really good clients. In fact, they're still clients because they're really good clients. In this chapter, I'm going to break the really great clients down into three categories but before I do I would have to highlight one common thread. Great clients use their broker because of the strengths that the broker has. They value the knowledge and experience that a broker can add to the investment relationship. Great clients also recognize that no one is perfect, broker included. The relationship with a great client therefore, becomes personal. This is a person that respects the broker for his strengths and understands his weaknesses. A broker can call this client any time with good news or bad, and feel totally comfortable.

So who are the great clients?

First there is THE PARTNER.

This client either knows a lot about investing or is learning very fast. This is probably the client that a broker spends the most time with. The partner may fall in to a few different sub-categories. They may be retired, having invested all their lives. They may be middle aged, having invested anywhere from five to twenty years or so. They may be the newly widowed, who have learned that their real career is now that of watching over the proceeds that their spouse left them through insurance. The income from their investments can be greater than the salary that they earn working. They may have inherited wealth. They may even be a former client's heir. Now the new investor has to oversee the inherited wealth. Finally, they may have cashed out of a corporation with retirement plan dollars that they now have to manage themselves.

Partners all have one thing in common. They're intelligent, savvy people but know how much they *don't* know. They acknowledge that they need financial help. They are articulate in defining their financial goals, both with the money they have, and that which they expect to end up with. They want the broker to be their partner. If they have a great idea for an investment they want to run it by him to see if it works. When the broker has a great idea, the partner knows enough to appreciate it and act quickly on it. If the broker's great idea isn't quite right for them, they know they can tell him. The broker can then move on to another client, while at the same time, constantly learning more about the partner's needs and financial desires. The Partner is a really great client.

There is THE SATURDAY AFTERNOON INVESTOR. I'm the "Saturday afternoon mechanic." How then, can I not appreciate the "Saturday afternoon investor." This investor is very much like the partner, with a major difference. To him investing isn't a necessity. It's a hobby. This client may have substantial assets or he may not, but he's a pleasure to work with. He really loves investing and spends considerable time working at it.

He is very knowledgeable. He really doesn't need the broker much of the time but when he does, he knows he does. If there's something that he doesn't understand about a particular investment, he won't hesitate to give his broker a call. If he likes it he'll buy it from the broker because that's who explained it to him. The broker knows he may not have all of Saturday's money. The broker doesn't need to have it all. When Saturday uses his broker, he pays him. When he doesn't need him, he probably trades with a discounter (a very low commission brokerage company that gives no financial advice). Saturday doesn't insult his broker by telling him about the discounter, but the broker probably knows about it. It doesn't bother him—to much. If the broker comes up with something that really excites Saturday, the broker will get the business. If it's really exciting, Saturday will buy some of it from the broker and perhaps go to the discounter for the balance.

Like the partner, Saturday can come up with some great ideas of his own, ideas his broker will review and then take to other clients.

The Saturday afternoon investor really doesn't take very much of a broker's time. He usually does his own homework. He calls in every so often for a report or two, maybe a recent chart on a particular stock of interest. When he does call, he knows exactly what he wants. Whether he calls his broker or his broker calls him, a decision is made quickly and each go on about their business.

The Saturday afternoon investor can be a really great client.

The third really great client is a little more complex. I call him the "DO IT" client. Different brokers may have different experiences with the "do it" client, but these clients usually have enough money to live very comfortably. Assets they hold may run in middle to high six figures or on into seven. Oddly enough they often view themselves as mediocre clients, hesitating to call the broker and take up his valuable time. If retired they have made, and if not they are making, substantial money through whatever endeavors they have chosen in life. Being bothered with the chore of watching the money, however, is not at all what drives them.

It takes your broker a few years to develop a Do It into a great client. This client may not know or care very much about investing money, but he does know a lot about trust. The broker may not even realize the client is a Do It, because the client is testing him to determine if such trust is really deserved. Once trusted, however, the broker can call this client with an idea. The answer he gets, is simple.

"Frank, if you think it's the right thing for me, Do it." And it's done. It may have taken all of three minutes on the phone to discuss two or three hundred thousand dollars of investments.

Does this client sound like every broker's dream? He is but it's not quite that simple. It's the closest thing for a broker, to having discretion (investing other peoples money without discussing it with them) that a non-discretionary broker will ever have. And with it comes responsibility.

Everything done in the Do It's account is the brokers responsibility. There's no "guilt sharing" here. It was all the broker's doing. That responsibility incidentally, is both moral and legal.

If this client ever takes his broker to arbitration or court because something went wrong, the broker can't exactly say "the client told me to do it." The fault win or lose, is 100% with the broker.

A conscientious broker really doesn't want to "blow up" this client. He watches the account like a hawk. The telephone call may have taken three minutes but the broker may have spent *hours* analyzing the account in order to reach a decision as to what should be done, if anything.

The broker probably gives this account more time than any other client. He manages this client's money truly as if it were his own. This is the account that the broker loses sleep over when it's down, and gets a real thrill out of, when it's making money.

In the hands of a good broker, the Do It client will make more money than any other client. The broker after all, is in a position to capitalize on opportunity and in the fast moving world of investments opportunity can come and go in moments. The Do It gets the first call. The broker doesn't have to console, cajole, sell, re-sell, debate, compare, analyze and hypothesize, in order to get the Do It to say yes.

Once he has finished calling all of his Do It clients, the broker moves on to calling his other clients. He allows them whatever time they need to make a decision, as the opportunity rapidly slips away.

If you are a Do It, you must be absolutely convinced that your broker is treating you fairly. If you mistakenly place your trust in a scavenger, you are a disaster waiting to happen. A broker with few scruples can destroy a Do It within months. Fortunately this rarely happens. The Do It may not be very savvy or very interested in investments, but he is extremely astute at reading people.

The Do It client knows he's paying for the service but it's immaterial to him. He may glance at his statements once every month or two, but he leaves the decisions to the broker. If the broker doesn't call he assumes everything is okay. If the broker calls he listens. If the broker recommends, he "Does It." No questions. No hesitation, For the broker that can handle this kind of responsibility, this is a really great client.

You may have noticed by now, that all of the really great clients have one extremely important attribute in common. They can make decisions. Instantly and without regret. Being a great client is not about how much money a client has. Whether they decide yes or no, great clients are decisive. You should also note that the faster the clients can make decisions, the higher they rank on the "call first with a good idea" list.

Are you a great client? If you are, you can count on the fact that your broker will never fire you. And he will say a little prayer for you each night, hoping that you never fire him.

As we think about the different brokers and clients we have seen, we should pause a moment for the obvious. These are the glaring examples. All of us at times, can be a little like each of them. The examples, however, should allow us more insight as to how different brokers function and how different clients relate to them. Hopefully, some of this insight will be helpful as you consider *your relationship*, with *your* broker.

My Broker left his company. What should I do?

18

My broker left his company. What should I do?

You wake up one Saturday morning. As you are having your mid-morning brunch, the telephone rings. It's George, your broker.

"Hi George," you begin as you wonder to yourself why he's calling at such a strange time. He usually hooks up to you during the week when he's in his office and the market is open. Your question is quickly answered.

"Tim, I'm calling you now to announce that I have left ABC brokerage company and am now affiliated with DEF. I'd really like to invite you to join me."

Depending on your relationship with both George and his old company this news may or may not be unsettling. Regardless, it comes as something of a surprise, perhaps even a complete shock to you. George had never mentioned that he was thinking of changing companies. You're a little insulted. Why didn't he say something Thursday when you last talked to him? He must have known he was going to move. Was he fired or what? It happened so quickly. Wait a minute. He *is* with a new company already. Yup, he had to know. He should have mentioned it.

You both talk for a while. He explains the reasons for his move, trying to convince you to transfer with him, to his new firm. He answers the few questions you can think to ask at the moment, and closes by asking you again to consider moving your account over with him. You end your conversation by telling him you will definitely consider the change, and you thank him as always for his call.

You mean a lot to George. You received one of his very first calls. Why didn't he tell you sooner? Why didn't he ask how *you* would feel about such a change? He *couldn't*, that's why.

In the securities brokerage business there is no such thing as giving a "two week notice." Changing firms is one of the most dramatic things a broker can do in his or her career and the decision doesn't come lightly. The broker in effect, fires his old company and hires a new one. It's almost always a Friday afternoon thing. Late afternoon. As with anyone who's been fired, the company usually doesn't take it very well! Even under the most amicable of circumstances it gets real nasty.

There is going to be a fight. "A Fight? Over what?" you ask. The "book." That's what.

Remember the book? Remember the debate over who owns the book? At the moment your broker said "So long" to his old company, that debate got intense. And the fight began over the book. Your broker couldn't breath a word of his impending change to you until he actually resigned his firm. Legally it would have seriously compromised his ability to defend his ownership of the book. He couldn't breath a word of it to his old firm either. They would have instantly fired him and commandeered his books. Then they would have begun calling his clients. Your broker couldn't take the actual books, but he did copy the pages, or he had the information about his clients on computer. Taking the books is almost always a no-no, legally. Taking the information? Well, that gets kind of grey. Those books are how your broker and his company make their money and it is serious business indeed.

The reason your broker resigned late on Friday afternoon is that it gave him the chance to contact you *first*. All through the weekend he contacted you and his other valuable clients. The company, on the other hand, still had to distribute the pages of the book to its remaining brokers before they got a chance to call anyone. The book had to be reviewed by the management. All of the favoritism, politic, and pure frenzy over the book came into focus in what some have said is the single most obnoxious and "client-indifferent" practice in the brokerage industry today—the *distribution of the book*.

Power brokers fight for their share. Those most favored by management receive the best clients, others receive the dregs. Fights break out over the book. Distribution of the pages in the book is, in almost every brokerage office, by complete management discretion. The manager quickly reviews each account (yours too) to determine its production capability. In this race against time for your dollars, it's conceivable that a rare and really superior manager might take the time necessary to try to determine the "fit" between a given client and the new broker assigned. Conceivable. But highly doubtful.

After the pages are distributed, the competition for your account begins in earnest. How hot the fight gets, often depends on the relationship that your broker had with those in his previous company. Sometimes, but not always (more often if the broker and his old company had a poor relationship) the old company will sue your broker, trying and occasionally succeeding in obtaining a restraining order that will restrict your broker from soliciting business from you for a certain period of time. More often, the brokers will settle for honest competition. May the best man and the best firm win. Medieval jousts were never fought with such veracity!

In many cases, again if your broker had good relationships at the old firm, the receiving broker at the old firm will not even call you for some period of time. He will allow your broker the professional courtesy of securing your account at his new firm. You shouldn't take this as a signal that the newly assigned broker doesn't care about you or your account. Feel free to call him if you wish to, or must for some reason. It's simply that your newly assigned broker is secure enough in his position to exercise such a courtesy to his old friend. After all it *may be him* some day.

Other newly assigned brokers attack the accounts like sharks in a feeding frenzy. Friendships mean nothing—there are dollars at stake! Some brokers will go so far as to suggest to you, what terrible investments your old broker placed you in and how poorly he handled your account. The new broker stands ready, of course, to "bail you out of the terrible mess you're in." Regardless of how the fight develops, the status of *your* page in the book is now very tenuous. You should act quickly to secure its well being. You should make a decision as quickly as you rationally can.

The old company thinks it owns your page in the book. Another broker has been assigned to your account. Who is this new guy? Who was your "luck of the draw" in all of this mayhem? Your old broker still lays claim to your page, and now, so does his new company.

Now is one of the most important times of all for you as a client, to remember who *really* owns the page—*you*! It really is after all, *your money*. You alone have the right to determine who handles it, no matter what happens at the firms.

You have choices here. They should be made knowledgeably and without intimidation from any of the various parties.

Your four choices are as follows. First, you can transfer to the new firm with your old broker. Second, you can stay with your old firm and whatever broker they assigned your account to. If you are unhappy with the broker that you "drew from the deck" during the hysteria and confusion of the distribution, you can exercise your third option. You can ask the manager of the old firm to assign another broker to you. This will make the manager very unhappy because, if you are a good client, he probably gave you to one of his favorites. Now he must tell this favored broker that you don't want him, and there are no other pages left to offer as a reward. Finally, you can choose this opportunity to shop for a completely new broker, at a completely new firm.

Many clients don't realize they have these choices. They think that, when the distribution happens, they are at the mercy of the company. Only the brokerage company can decide what broker is best for them. It's simply not so. Probably the very last consideration (if it even is a consideration) given during the distribution, is "what broker would be best for this or that individual client."

So what *was* your relationship with your old broker? Was it a good one. If it was a really good one, yours should be an easy decision. You always trusted him. Trust him now. He's done well for you. If he changed companies for what ever reasons, you can still rely on his decision. You trusted him when he recommended investments. Why second guess him when he now recommends a new firm affiliation. It's a simple choice, and you sign off on the transfer papers you received in the mail just after you got his call. These papers instruct the old firm to transfer your account immediately to your broker at his new company.

Was the broker the only broker you ever had? Were you new to the game when you came to him. Has he treated you well? Perhaps he has, but now you wonder what it would be like to try another broker. "If it ain't broke, don't fix it." You liked this guy? Stay with him. Experiment someplace else. The handling of your money is no place to play games.

Perhaps you've had or still have a few different brokers. How does this guy compare to them? If he's good, stay with him. If you really haven't been happy with him, you shouldn't have been dealing with him anyway.

Maybe it's a matter of convenience. You think to yourself, "Changing accounts to the new firm is gonna' be a pain. I'll just stay at the old firm and take my chances. Brokers are all the same anyway."

Change is always a nuisance but now you *have* to change. You either have to change *firms* to stay with your broker, or you have to change *brokers* to stay with the old firm. The biggest change is a change in brokers, not companies. Transferring your account from one brokerage company to another is no big deal. This is a business of relationships. If you stay with your old friend at a new company that's a very minor change. If you elect to stay with the old firm and accept whatever new broker they gave you, it's a *major* change. It may be a good change or it may be a bad change, but it *is* a *major* change. If you come to the conclusion that you really liked your old guy but changing will just be too much trouble then fine. Stay with the old company and take your chances. This is one instance where complacency or procrastination can really hurt you, but it's your money.

Some clients, usually not very good ones, see this development as a golden opportunity. They decide to transfer *some* of their business to the old guy and keep some of their assets with their newly assigned broker. They figure they'll sort of play them off against each other and have two brokers instead of one.

It's not a good idea. Your broker is a realist. He knows his clients may have other brokers and he can accept that. But he really doesn't want to find himself in competition with an *old friend* over your account.

These guys will still be tipping a few beers together down at the local watering hole after the initial frenzy of the distribution wears off. The last thing either of them wants to talk about is your account that they now share. Both brokers would have to be desperate for business, to be content with such an arrangement. Both of the brokers will resent your desire to play them against each other. The least desperate broker will fire you or they both will fire you, and then your choice will have been made for you. You either got the most desperate broker of the two, or no broker at all.

Why did your old broker leave his firm? If you don't know, ask him. Then ask your newly assigned broker. If your newly assigned broker won't tell you, that's a positive indication for both your old broker *and* your new one. If the new one suggests that your old guy was a real bum, that's definitely a plus for your old broker. Any broker who bad mouths another broker in his first contact with the client, is out of line, plain and simple. Criticism of brokers is best left to clients and industry regulators. They are both very good at it!

You need to find out if there are any serious problems with your newly assigned broker. Call the (800) 289-9999 NASD number. Hopefully, you already called them about your old broker and were comfortable with the response. They can tell you if your new broker has some nasty little problems sticking to his license. Again, it's public knowledge and it's yours for the asking.

Okay. So you've talked this situation over with both brokers. You've called the NASD. Both guys are squeaky clean. You're leaning toward the transfer to the new company so you can stay with your old "comfort factor" but wait. What about his new company? Who are they? Do you know anything about them?

It's nice to feel good about the broker that's been handling your finances with you for the last X years but it's nicer still to know that he *did* pick a firm that will support both he and you, in your continuing efforts towards wealth. Perhaps now it's time to refer back to Chapter VII and review once again "Who does your broker work for."

Keep in mind one thing though. It's the broker that makes your relationship, not the firm. Don't get hung up over little things like statement format or whether the firm has this or that little service that you happen to like. The underlying investments will still ring true regardless of what kind of statement you receive. There are some really good brokers who work for companies that offer very little in the way of "client services." Would you rather deal with someone who really knows a lot about this investment stuff, or a novice at a company that allows you to call in for your account balance every night at midnight. I don't know about you but I'm in the business and I know what my answer would be.

Another question you are completely justified in raising to your old friend is this. "How long do you think you'll be staying with *this* new company?" Sure he's changed companies. But is it going to happen every year or two? How long was he with the old firm? Why did he change? If your broker felt he had to change affiliations to be able to conduct his business the way he wanted to, there's no telling for sure if he'll have to do it again. Changes in branch management, or in company philosophies can present concerns to your broker that he didn't anticipate.

The best answer you could hope for would be an honest one. If he hopes to stay with his new company forever, but reserves the right to change again, you can't ask for much more. As long as he continues to look out for your best interests.

How good a client are you? This might be a good time to re-asses yourself. You can bet your old broker has reassessed you. When your broker changes companies he views it as a great time to "clean up his book." No broker wants to lose a good client but when he switches companies, it's a perfect time for him to give up clients he doesn't really need. Part of that eighty percent that with luck, throws off two percent of his business while providing him with fifty percent of his aggravation? He will definitely leave those clients at his old firm where they will be given to the newest, most inexperienced brokers.

The bottom line is this. When you ask someone to help you handle your money, it gets very personal. You may confide things to your broker that you wouldn't tell your mother or your spouse. That big company can't possibly care about you as much as your individual broker does.

If your broker changes companies and you like him, stay with him. You probably won't be sorry if you stay with him but you could end up real sorry if you don't.

My Stock Broker left the Business! What should I do?

19

My Stock Broker Left the Business! What do I do?

You are probably not going to be dealing with the same broker for the rest of your life.

Those of you who have been fortunate enough to have dealt with the same broker for lets say ten years, are lucky indeed. Fifteen years. Count your blessings and pray for him every night before you go beddy by! Twenty years? Fantastic. You are among the rare few.

The fact of life is, that the daily war with the boredom, finicky markets and the wrenching efforts of trying to preserve your money (not to mention his own) rips away at your broker's very soul. Sales quotas and pressure to produce more commissions only add to the stress. Brokers burn out.

Brokers as we have noted, come from many walks of life. Few indeed are those who can survive the daily trauma of this business. Fewer still those that thrive on it and even fewer carry it to the bitter end, ie. retirement. Even if they do, by definition of the word "retirement" they're gone. Unless you die before your broker leaves the business you will not have the same broker for the rest of your life. This business will test the mettle of even the strongest personalities and very often the business will claim the victory.

So you get another call, later in the evening this time. It's not from your broker either. It's from another broker. It starts out like a "Cold Call" but can end up striking you with anything from concern to absolute fear.

"Hi! Good evening sir, is this Mr.- uh, Terajakoliski?

"Terry-jako-lipski you repeat from force of habit, pronouncing your difficult name. Yes it is, what do you want?"

"Good evening sir. My name is Jerry Hopscotch and I wanted to take a moment of you time to introduce myself as your new broker."

Wait a minute. What's this "my new broker stuff?"

He goes on. "Mr Fitzholder has left the firm sir, and your account has just been assigned to me. I'd like to get together with you sometime soon to review your portfolio. I see your holding 1200 shares of Whoolawhats stock."

"Whoa," you think to yourself. This isn't just another cold call. This guy knows I'm holding Whoolawhats and he's probably going to embarrass me over it. What happened to Ricky anyway?"

"What happened to Ricky?"

"Well sir, Richard Fitzholder has left us and your account has been assigned to me."

A pause in the dialogue for a moment. Lots of heavy breathing on both ends of the line.

You are now a victim of the D-I-S-T-R-I-B-U-T-I-O-N again!

I have previously described the distribution as one of the lowest forms of brokerage activity that could ever possibly be devised by mankind, but wait! There is an upside to the practice. If you have a brokerage account with someone somewhere, you will probably never be *without* a broker unless you choose to be. You will always have a broker to talk to—to enter absolutely necessary trades. Whether your broker leaves for another firm, leaves the business or leaves mother earth, his office is going to insure that should you need immediate attention, you'll get it. Your account will always be handled by someone in the event disaster or amazing good fortune should strike you during this transition period. If during *this* period the office can't help you out, you really better be sure to find another place to handle your account.

So your instant gut reaction is, "Where did Fitz go?"

"I'm not really sure sir. They tell me he's left the business. Your account has been reassigned to me and I just wanted to call you to let you know. Really liked Fitz. Great guy!" This guy hated Fitz but he'd be crazy to tell you now, how he felt.

"Uh Oh! Fitz has left for parts unknown and now this guy Hopscotch is calling me and everything I have he already knows about." You pause.

"You don't know where he went?"

"Not really sir. He walked in this morning and said good-by to everyone. He mentioned something about grass skirts in Tahiti."

Be cautious here. Did Fitz really leave the business or did he simply switch companies and you haven't heard from him yet?

If he switched you'll know it pretty soon. You'll hear from him quickly enough.

If he dropped out of the business it's different. What do you do?

Talk to Mr. Hopscotch for a few minutes. He very well may be your new broker. He already has your statement in front of him along with your page in the book. He may already know more about you than your spouse, your mother or your favorite bar tender. Spend a few minutes with him and get to know him but don't make any hasty decisions. Fitz may show up. If he doesn't, then you have alternatives. You might end the conversation with Hopscotch by saying something like this.

"Well I really always felt good about Fitz's recommendations and I'm not about to do anything right now. In fact I would like to hear from him before I make any decisions at all concerning investments. If you hear from him, ask him to contact me if he can."

Obviously, one of a few different things happened with Fitz.

If he did switch companies he couldn't contact you before he left and that may be something you'll want to consider. You may very well be on his list for a call when he recovers from his initial exhaustion.

If he really did quit the business and if he cared about you at all, you already know it. He called you himself and told you he was leaving.

He might have gotten fired. Maybe his production wasn't up to snuff. He had three bad months in a row because he didn't recommend to you and his other clients, bad investments that his company was pushing. The commissions on it would have helped him meet his quotas and curried some favor. A new manager or less likely perhaps even his old one simply gave him his walking papers. Maybe he got entirely disgusted with his branch operation and told them all where to go.

Perhaps he took his bride of twenty years and bought a grass roof condo on a Chilean beach.

The bottom line is this. If you don't hear from good old Fitz in a couple of weeks you can assume your relationship didn't really mean much to him or that he simply dropped out. In either case you're on your own.

If Fitz should give you a call, give him your undivided attention. It means he cares enough about you to let you know what happened. If he left the business and he thinks enough about you to call you, he may have some interesting things to say.

He obviously will tell you what happened and why he left but he also may make some recommendations to you. If he doesn't, your objective is to ask some very important questions of him.

1. Who's Hopscotch? Can I trust him?

2. Who else in your office might I request? Remember, just because you got assigned to one broker doesn't mean you have to stay with him. Fitz may recommend you a broker. Unlike the firm, he *knows* how you did business and he knows how the broker's in the office do business. He is probably a much better person to ask for a recommendation than some office manager you never met that may have handed out your page of the book to whomever happened to be leading in a sales contest at the time.

3. "Can I have your home or new office number? I'd like to keep in touch from time to time. We had some really good laughs together." Fitz may be retired but he still probably knows more about the markets than most relatives or friends you have. It might not be a bad idea to tap into that knowledge from time to time. Fritz may be flattered that you asked. Most brokers are "people persons" and keeping in touch with you will be a "fun thing" for him, especially if you had a good relationship.

4. "How was that office anyway?" Should you still be comfortable doing business with them?

Keep in mind something else. Your former broker may not be able to contact all of his former clients but if you can contact him he'll probably be happy enough to talk to you. Don't hesitate to give him a call—at home, his new office, in Tahiti or anywhere you can reach him. After all, you fed this guy. You're entitled to make the call and he probably won't mind a bit. He may very well be flattered that you took the time to locate him.

Here's a suggestion that may save you countless hours of aggravation and pay for the cost of this book several times over! Don't wait for Fitz to leave! Your broker wants to know who he can talk to if something should happen to you. He may have asked you directly or he may already know, from beneficiaries you have listed on your retirement account or from current relationships he has with your family. His need for such information isn't altogether altruistic. If you should meet with misfortune he would very much like to retain the assets in your account.

Aren't you entitled to the same if something should happen to your broker?

"Fitz, I know this is kind of sensitive, and I've been very happy working with you but if something should happen to you, who should I ask for as a new broker? You know me better than your manager does. Is there someone you would recommend that would work with me as well as you have?"

Fitz may chuckle a couple of times. He has probably *never* been asked this question but he has probably thought about it from time to time. It shouldn't take him more than thirty seconds to give you a name and if he is confident about his relationship with you he shouldn't hesitate for an instant.

Fitz knows a lot of brokers and from them, has developed a close circle of broker friends. These are usually his close broker friends because they handle their business in much the same manner as he does. Since you are happy with Fitz, you stand a very good chance of being similarly happy with any of his close broker friends—whether or not they happen to work at his firm. He knows you and he knows them. You simply couldn't ask for a better recommendation so why shouldn't you—while you can?

If your broker really did burn out, if he did quit the business because he simply couldn't take it any more, he may not want to hear from you. He may not want to hear from anyone or anything that would bring back the frustration of struggling on a daily basis to fend off the markets, make clients good money and make a few uncertain dollars of his own in the process.

Don't take it personally. You have remedies open to you if you didn't get around to asking him for a recommendation while you were working with him. You already have a new broker. Who knows? He may turn out to be a great guy with superior ideas and your new relationship will grow. You can request another broker in the office if this is not the case. Obviously, you can still take your business to another firm. This may be the ideal time to "shop around."

Nothing is forever. If you had a very good broker, be thankful for pleasant memories and go find another one. If your old relationship was less than satisfactory but you somehow never got around to changing the situation, fine. Now you're forced to.

In either case now that you know what kind of client you are and know what kind of broker to look for, the job should be a little easier. What ever you do don't just settle for whomever they give you. If you do you'll end up with another less than satisfactory relationship that you never get around to changing.

The Ideal
Broker for You.

20

The Ideal Broker for You

One of the really big frustrations in this world is that none of us are perfect. The guy upstairs seems to take all of the really perfect people leaving the rest of us to suffer with our own deficiencies.

Occasionally he leaves a few "almost perfect" people down here for us to look up to, admire, and perhaps even strive to be like, but mostly we eat humble pie down here. In the financial business we eat it a lot more than we'd like to!

No broker is perfect. There is no such thing as the ideal broker just as there is no such thing as the ideal client.

The broker you eventually work with will be much more ideal for you however, if you think about the selection process a little bit more. Concentrate on the different styles of brokering, relating them specifically to what type of client you are. We all know about personal "chemistry." It goes a long way in the client-broker relationship. Here are some thoughts that may lead you to a better match—to a broker you can be most comfortable with.

There's an expression in the business. "A broker's book eventually takes on his own personality." It means that a broker's clients usually have similar personality characteristics to those of their broker. It's a natural thing. In a highly confidential relationship you are probably going to trust someone more if they view situations much like you do.

If you are a political conservative you may not be best served by having a liberal as your broker. Your conversations will eventually take a well deserved break from the tedium of investing and turn to other things. Unless you have a salesman who's political persuasion shifts instantly to that of his client you don't want to end up disliking this person for his or her different beliefs do you?

Different ethnic or even religious groups often (not always) feel more comfortable with brokers of the same persuasion. Right or wrong, no one can force you to be politically or socially correct when you select your broker. Gender may be an issue. Some of us feel more comfortable discussing our finances with the same sex, and others feel more secure with the opposite sex but which ever way you feel, "comfort" is the operative word. "Comfort" and "Competence."

Time is a valuable resource. As you select a broker or work with the one you have, it might be useful to think about where he invests his time. Different brokers invest their time differently and different clients have different needs. Who might work best with whom?

If you find it really difficult to make investment decisions, you may very well belong with a salesman broker. Why? He will definitely help you make decisions. He will inundate you with information about the investment he is presenting to you and probably has more ways to make you feel comfortable about it than you could ever imagine. You might be one of our Analyst clients. You want all of the information available about any given situation. The salesman has it—right there on the script card in front of him. You may be Thrifty. The salesman is very good at "arm bending" and if you are hesitant to purchase an investment because of the cost you are definitely going to need some "arm bending" to get you to do the right thing.

There is another type of client that the salesman usually does very well with. The "New" client. If you never invested before and are nervous about the idea of placing your hard earned dollars into an area that is totally foreign to you, go see a salesman. He will give you just the information that you need to allow you to feel all warm and cozy. No more, no less. He will also spend as much time as he needs to with you, to overcome any objections or concerns you may have. If you are nervous or inexperienced investor you probably don't need an intellect. The intellect will insure you have so much information that you leave the office trembling in a pouring sweat! It will be superior information but with luck you'll understand ten percent of it and that other ninety percent may keep you from doing the right thing forever!

Spend a couple of years with your salesman first, then search out one of the other types of broker as you grow more comfortable with the basic concepts.

The salesman invests almost all of his time in the continuing effort to find new clients. It's an excellent use of time. Nothing brings in commission dollars in the brokerage business like a new client. If you are a new client the salesman will spend inordinate amounts of time with you. As the relationship matures however, you might find him less and less available. He's busy spending his time on other new clients. The salesman usually lets his company or others decide which investments to select from. He doesn't have much time for serious research. He often even lets others design his sales pitch.

What about that intellect? Great broker for you Partners, Saturday Afternoon Investors and Just Do Its. You need someone who has in depth knowledge of your investments and is constantly watching things you never even thought about as he makes his recommendations to you. The Analysts will also come to quickly recognize the intellect as a peer and will be comfortable dealing with his extra base of knowledge.

If you are a Time Taker, the intellect may be just the person for you. He enjoys spending an hour or two on the phone impressing you with his competence. Just don't abuse the privilege. He *is* there to make money — both for you and himself.

The intellect spends his time researching. He researches everything. The investment, the news as it applies to the investment, the news as it doesn't even apply to the investment. Knowledge is what pays this broker and he spends a great deal of his time acquiring it.

The investment consultant or money manager needs a Do It, a Partner, a Saturday Afternooner and a decision maker for a client. If you are one of these clients, you may be in very good hands with the investment consultant. This broker is probably also more likely to take on family and friends. Like the intellect he doesn't rely very much on others to make his investment decisions for him. He does his own research and is comfortable with it. He usually doesn't research to the depth of the intellect but he doesn't just take someone's word for something either.

Your investment consultant is basically a money manager in broker's clothing. He spends his time on the accounts he already has, taking on new accounts as they come to him. If you have an investment consultant you can expect your account to be handled somewhat differently than other brokers. No dust settles on your statement. It is reviewed constantly to insure that it is performing to the maximum level possible. You can anticipate a fairly active account if you have this broker but you can also expect that to the best of his or her ability you will be in the best possible investments at any given time. This broker has little use for ideas that don't work out. He will sell under performing investments out of your account very quickly.

Your investment consultant (along with his intellect buddy) will also probably anticipate developing changes earlier than other brokers. He may call you and tell you to get out of utilities while everyone else is calling you and telling you that it's the "only place to be." These brokers are independent thinkers. They don't follow the masses.

There's no secret as to where the specialist spends his time. On his specialty of course. His chosen area of investment is almost by definition intricate and complex. It requires a lot of time to learn the various aspects of the specialty area and to develop the level of expertise that few others have. Does it pay? You bet. When you need to know everything there is to know about your Limited Partnership or Commodity Futures there is no where else to turn. You will have to become a Do It client when you work with the Specialist. You will never know all that he knows about his given area of expertise.

The Specialist can make an excellent "second broker" for any client. He will rarely ask you for the rest of your assets although if he works for a full service firm he will handle them in much the same way as the salesman does—for the same reason. Time.

There are a couple of other things you may want to consider before selecting your broker.

Is your broker secure in what he does—both financially and in the business. Your broker doesn't have to be rich. If he won the lottery he probably wouldn't be your broker any more. But you do want to get the feeling that he has a few bucks of his own. Nothing can teach someone how to invest better than investing their own money. It's not paper money any more—it's real. You certainly don't need a broker that can't afford to pay his own rent if he has a slow month or two. You can almost bet he'll find a way for you to pay it for him. You also don't want a broker who has to worry about whether he's going to get fired if he has a bad month or two—especially if he works in a high pressure office.

You want your broker to be comfortable. Not because you're concerned about his well being. Rather, because it's *your* broker and you're concerned about *your* well being.

Should your broker be your friend? Should you expect him to be your friend? The "friends and family" situation is already established but should the normal client-broker relationship grow into a long personal friendship?

Probably not. If you expect a close friendship with your broker you may be making a mistake. Obviously any long term relationship between people will grow stronger with time and a good relationship between broker and client is imperative. But don't let it grow to a social friendship. You and your broker may be doing each other a disservice if you do. There are times when even the most low-pressure broker is going to have to "strong arm" you to get you to do what needs to be done. You may want to actually hate this person for awhile. There are times when your broker is going to be wrong about and investment—and it will cost you money. You may want to hate this person for awhile longer. There may be a time when you realize you just don't see eye to eye any more. He may fire you—or you may fire him. Do you want to hate your friend forever?

What I'm suggesting here is controversial. Not every one would agree with me and in fact a good many people would probably disagree. Many brokers go out of their way to "schmooze it up" with their clients, trying to make them best friends. It *may* just be an effort to instill false confidence.

"My good friend Bill wouldn't take advantage of me, would he?" Friendships made under such false premise are not enduring.

An occasional social gathering where the broker client relationship remains completely clear and unadulterated is one thing but unless you both view the rewards of the potential friendship as greater than those of the client-broker relationship, the business relationship is probably the better one.

Let your broker be your broker. Let your friends be your friends.

Our focus thus far has been to explore your broker and your relationship specifically with him or her. We have looked at the different styles of brokering and some of the different groups of clients that they work with.

Lets look at some broader issues now. There are changes taking place in the financial industry that smart investors should be aware of. You can be sure your broker is currently watching these issues closely in order to protect both his interests and those of his valued clients.

Legal and Compliance Issues.

21

Legal and Compliance Issues

I'm not a lawyer and this chapter isn't designed as a comprehensive analysis of the legalities governing the securities industry. As a client, though, you do want to have a general understanding as to what recourse you have, should a dispute with your broker arise. As a smart investor you should also be aware of how some of these issues can affect your broker's performance and for that matter, the performance of your account.

There is one thing that absolutely fascinates me about the brokerage business. Once a brokerage account has been opened and the account documents have been signed, almost all of the transactions the broker and his client enter into are verbal.

In the securities business, millions of dollars in transactions can be handled verbally, either on the phone or in person. There is no "statute of frauds," requiring that each buy or sell order be reduced to writing, with both parties signing separate agreements each time a transaction is made.

If you call your broker and tell him to buy you a million dollars worth of tax free bonds, and he agrees to do so, you have made a contract with him. It's a legally enforceable contract. You agreed to pay him for the purchase of the bonds. He agreed to buy the bonds for you. When he buys the bonds, you are legally on the hook for the million bucks. If he doesn't buy the bonds, he's on the hook for whatever you might lose, should the bonds rise in value while you don't own them. The only little nitty gritty problem either of you would have, would be proving who said what to whom.

Problems of misunderstanding in the brokerage business, are most often solved by a silly little concept called "good faith." It's the old fashioned "handshake rule." In order for this concept to work, though, brokers and clients must feel pretty comfortable with each other.

If a broker accepts your offer to buy the bonds, he must be quite sure you can and will pay for them. If you agree for him to purchase the bonds for you, you had better be confident that he'll do it. The concept of "good faith" suggests that both of you will do what's best to make the situation right, should a misunderstanding develop. It's amazing how well this simple system of honor and trust still works— even in modern day America.

As a client, however, you should know that there *is* a "paper trail" of every transaction done through your broker. You do get those confirmations. Those little slips of paper that describe each transaction you make? Don't just throw them in a file and forget about them. They are written record of the entire transaction.

Confirmations are always marked either "solicited" or "unsolicited." If the trade was solicited, it means the broker either suggested the transaction, or helped you make your decision about it. If the confirmation is unsolicited, it states that you alone as client made the decision to buy or sell.

When your broker enters a trade for you, paperwork takes place. Your broker enters a "ticket" into his system.

This is his actual order to the trading desk or exchange floor, where the sale actually takes place. It instructs the traders to buy or sell a security for your account. The ticket is either hand written by the broker, or more likely these days, is entered on his computer screen. Hard copy confirmations are generated to both broker and client, when the trade is completed.

The ticket, whether by hand or computer, contains all of the specific instructions to the trader that will complete the transaction for you. It includes your name, account number, the description of the securities to be bought or sold, and the quantity of same. It is here, that the broker indicates whether the trade was solicited or not. These tickets are kept by the brokerage company as written evidence of the transaction.

When you, the client, receive your confirmation, you should review it immediately for accuracy. You should also review your statements specifically for trading activity. There have been instances of unscrupulous brokers or firms grabbing confirms before they're mailed to the clients. Most firms protect against this but if a trade was made, it will appear on your statement. If you find a discrepancy, contact your broker at once and try to resolve it. In most cases you will be able to fix the problem on the telephone but if you feel you are not getting satisfaction, write a letter to the firm immediately, detailing your side of the story. Your letter will then be added to the "paper trail" of the transaction for future reference.

Lets simplify this. If you have an argument with your broker about a transaction, you don't want the only written evidence to be *his* ticket and your *unanswered* confirmation, when the attorneys get around to it. It may be a verbal business, but attorneys, judges and arbitrators like to see "hard copy."

Ninety nine times out of a hundred (actually more like nine hundred ninety nine times out of a thousand) the good faith effort will get your dispute resolved. But there are occasional problems.

Honest misunderstandings do come up. There are also unscrupulous brokers and unscrupulous clients. If you have a disagreement with your broker about a transaction, you do have recourse.

Your first step was to call your broker. Your second step was to document your side of the story in writing and send it to your broker with a copy to his office manager. Your third step is to call the broker's branch office manager, seeking resolution. Depending on the office manager and/or the nature of the complaint, you may or may not get your problem resolved at this level.

If you still get no satisfaction, your next call (followed up by letter) will be to the company headquarters. Most large brokerage companies have departments to handle just such disputes. They will review all of the paperwork involved in the transaction and try to come up with a resolution for you. If after all of this you are still unsatisfied, you have a choice. You can either give up, or you can pursue the matter legally. If you are dealing with a reputable firm, you may decide now, to give up. The firm knows whether you have a valid claim or not. If your claim is valid, the firm will usually (not always) find a way to fix it, rather than suffer a lawsuit or arbitration claim.

There are two types of legal pursuit available to clients in the securities industry. The first is a lawsuit and the second is arbitration. Both are costly and very uncomfortable for both the client and the broker.

If you have not signed an "arbitration clause" when you opened your brokerage account, you are entitled to file a lawsuit, taking your case directly to the courts. You will most likely need an attorney to do this and of course, the brokerage company will incur the legal expense of defending itself.

In an environment where millions of verbal transactions occur annually, brokerage companies have taken steps to protect themselves from the inevitable problems that will occur. How do they do this? They have their clients sign arbitration clauses when the account is opened.

Most companies today require clients to sign an arbitration clause when opening any but the most basic of accounts. In the arbitration clause the client agrees to settle any disputes through arbitration as opposed to a lawsuit. The client agrees not to sue the brokerage company.

Debate rages on as to whether these required clauses are fair to clients or not. Some would suggest that the client has a better chance of winning a dispute in court. Others would suggest that arbitration is fairer to all parties because those hearing the argument are more familiar with securities problems. Both sides are probably right. A client would probably have a better chance in court, where a jury of citizens totally ignorant of the securities business, would weigh the evidence. It is probably fairer to all parties, however, if knowledgeable people are judging the evidence. If as a client, you seek only a fair resolution to any potential problem, you should have no hesitation signing an arbitration clause. You are simply agreeing to have knowledgeable but disinterested parties resolve your claim. You *will get* a fair hearing. You can still hire an attorney to present your case if you wish to, but going to arbitration will probably save you and your brokerage company a bundle in lawyers fees.

Don't think for a minute think that the arbitration panel will be biased in favor of the broker. The arbitrators can be members of one of the various stock exchanges, one of the security industry regulatory boards, or even from a disinterested brokerage firm. They represent the industry and are usually selected for their concern about keeping its image above reproach. If your broker is wrong, he will sweat and you will win.

If, of course, you are a client who would prefer winning your case whether the outcome is fair or not, *don't ever* sign an arbitration clause.

So how does a client (or broker) win an arbitration or a lawsuit? All of those little pieces of paper, that's how. Documentation is everything. In a world without written agreements, the best that the arbitrators (or any court of law) can attempt to do, is to determine the facts of the case. The broker or client with the best documentation has the obvious edge.

You should know that the little pieces of paper these guys look at, won't be just the ones from *your* particular transaction. The broker may have to provide documents on any or all of his past transactions. Most security trades, for example, are solicited. If your broker is claiming your trade or trades were unsolicited (they were your idea alone) and your confirmations were so marked, the judges may want to see *other* confirmations, from his *other* clients. If an unusually large number of those confirmations are also unsolicited, the broker is going to have to explain that. He probably won't have much fun trying.

When your broker calls you, make a quick hand written note of the conversation and throw it in your "broker file." Most brokers jot down conversations, either on computer or by hand. If you ever have the misfortune of going to court or arbitration, those notes will be invaluable. It's simple. The best documentation wins.

As a client, if you are honest and forthright in your dealings, you should have no qualms about signing an arbitration agreement. Your broker should have no concern in explaining the arbitration agreement to you. If you don't want to sign it, fine. The broker shouldn't want you for a client. You probably aren't interested in fairness and he doesn't need that kind of aggravation.

It may be a handshake business but arbitration claims and lawsuits are being filed with ever increasing frequency. To some it would seem that right or wrong hardly matters any more. More important to many is "can I get a settlement?" Lawsuits are expensive, especially for the defendant. The plaintiff can usually retain an attorney on contingency whereby legal fees are paid only if the suit is successful. The plaintiff, therefor has no financial risk in bringing the lawsuit (or arbitration case). The plaintiff's lawyer, fully recognizing that he doesn't get paid at all if the suit is unsuccessful, will do everything possible to insure a paycheck—and what better target than a brokerage firm with all those deep pockets. The defendant in the matter, pays regardless. Defense attorneys rarely work on contingency and hardly ever work for nothing. Because of this, settlements begin to look very attractive to any defendant in a civil case. Your broker knows this and it presents him with a very unique concern. If he is sued or brought to arbitration and the firm decides it is more economically feasible to settle the case, it still goes on the broker's records. These records are both private to his firm and public. They're the ones that you hear about when you call that NASD telephone number we mentioned earlier.

This places your broker and his firm (along with many other members of our society) in a no-win situation. It's not just about dollars—it's about his formal record whether he was right or wrong. He and his firm must be extraordinarily careful about how they do business with their clients and even if they are, they are still at risk.

That's nice, but what does it mean to you, the client, and more specifically, the performance of your account?

There are various ways that your broker can defend himself against frivolous claims but two of the best are the reasonableness of the client and the suitability of the investment he recommended. They both fall under the broader "know your client" rule. One of these he can document, the other is more judgmental. When a broker buys an investment for you, whether solicited or not, it's documented. But how does he know that it was suitable for you? If you are an established client of his, he should know your basic financial situation and be able to make that call very quickly. He also knows and has dealt with you for a while and has already established in his mind that you are a reasonable person.

If you are a new client to the broker, he knows neither of these two things and you immediately become a greater risk to him. Most brokers today will interview new clients rather extensively in order to determine what their financial resources are and what investments might be suitable for them. Most brokerage companies have guidelines concerning minimum information that must be taken during these interviews. If you are uncomfortable sharing your financial situation with the broker (as many people are), he simply may not do business with you. It's not that he doesn't appreciate or respect your desire for privacy. It's simply that the rules, regulations and lawyers have forced him to pry deeply into your situation in order to establish "suitability." Put another way, these various entities have determined that you as a client are not responsible enough to determine what investments might be right for you. The broker bears that burden. We may not like the premise but we don't control it either.

What is suitability? What does it mean? Simply put, an investment is suitable if the client is willing and able to assume the risk of the particular investment. Many are willing. Fewer may be able. Perhaps a few examples would help.

An option, as we have noted earlier, is a high risk but potentially very rewarding investment. If a client has liquid assets of say, four hundred thousand dollars (it could be more or less), is gainfully employed and wishes to purchase an option for say, two thousand dollars, she can probably afford to lose it. It is not going to dramatically affect her lifestyle, win, lose or draw. If on the other hand, a young couple with ten thousand dollars to their name, which they happen to be saving toward a house, wants to place it all on the same option with the hope of buying the house cash rather than having to take out a mortgage, it's not suitable. They will probably lose the house.

If a retired couple has an account worth a few hundred thousand, of which fifty percent is in options, it's not suitable either. They can't go back and earn it again and if they lose their money, it is going to dramatically affect their lifestyle. These are glaring examples but it gets more subtle.

Tax free bonds are a staple of conservative investing. The income they pay is tax free but they pay less income than taxable bonds because of this. If a client decides he wants to buy a few thousand dollars of tax free bonds and his tax bracket is not high enough to justify the benefit of the tax free income, it could be construed as unsuitable. Hmm. Don't expect your broker to buy you just any old investment you may want to buy. It may not be suitable in his eyes, even if it seems fine to you. And he simply can't afford the risk.

In the interview process with the new client, the broker is also is beginning to determine in his own mind, whether or not this potential client is a reasonable person. (He is always re-assessing his current clients for any possible changes.) If the client has unrealistic expectations about the investment she is begging to buy, she probably is not acting reasonably and she probably is not going to buy it through that broker.

Active accounts (accounts that buy and sell investments often) can make more money—for the client and the broker. Why hold an under performing security when it can be sold and the money re-invested in one that is performing?

Active accounts are also a red flag to the broker, his firm, and the lawyers. The activity can be construed as "churning," the practice of buying and selling strictly so the broker can make more commission. Some clients (many very savvy ones) like their accounts to be active. Others don't and still others don't have a clue as to whether it is active or not. If your account is turning over more than two times a year (you have bought and sold securities worth two times the value of the account) you can consider it quite active. The simple fact that your account is active may not be a bad thing. If you are making money (the total account balance is going up) or saving money in bad markets (the total account balance is flat or down but is performing better than the overall markets) you can probably attribute the superior performance to the activity. Your broker is making money but you are too. If, on the other hand, your active account is dropping rapidly or is dramatically under performing the markets, your broker is making money and you are not. You may have a serious problem and you should act quickly to freeze the activity of the account until you have absolutely satisfactory reasons for the results you are witnessing.

Whether good or bad, active accounts are a red flag. Knowing this, your broker wants to be very comfortable with the personalities behind those active accounts. You as a client should also be very comfortable with the broker behind your active account.

A broker who is very good at making money with active accounts will often wait until he knows the client very well. He will start the account off slowly until he feels that his client is comfortable with the performance and reasonable with expectations. If you are a client that likes your account managed actively, you are probably much better off with a broker that you have known for some time. You shouldn't expect to walk into a new broker and immediately enjoy the profits of an active account that is well managed.

Your broker's firm has what is called a "compliance department." Within various firms it may operate differently but basically this is the department responsible for keeping your broker out of court and arbitration, while at the same time insuring that the broker and the firm are in compliance with the many state and federal regulations that pertain to the industry.

This department is your broker's best friend although most brokers would rarely acknowledge it. All of the various rules, regulations and policies that they police can severely restrict the broker's freedom in the way he does business. In doing so they oft times inhibit the commissions he can make and more importantly to you the client, the profits that his clients make. "Police," in fact, would be a great way to describe the relationship between your broker and his compliance department. You love your local cop when she comes to your aid while stranded on the side of the road or perhaps when you get injured at home and need to get to the hospital fast. They're great people to have happen by, if your pre-occupied some night in the shadier part of town getting mugged. But you're going to hate them when they issue you a traffic fine for sailing through that stop sign you didn't happen to see or when they pull you over for doing fifty on a main road, through a school zone posted at thirty five. If you had slowed to thirty five through that zone, a Mack truck would have rear-end you— and then you'd need the cop to untangle you from your Fiat. It's a love-hate relationship with the compliance departments but they have their jobs to do and they have to do them.

What really makes their jobs difficult (not to mention the job of the broker) is the outside regulations they are required to enforce.

It's getting harder and harder for your broker to make a living in the financial business he's in. Regulation is killing him—and it's costing you, the client, big dollars. Regulation in the securities business comes primarily from two sources. The first is governmental. The Securities and Exchange Commission. The second is from the supposedly self administered industry regulation arm, the National Association of Securities Dealers (the NASD).

It's almost impossible for your broker to advertise his business anymore. Almost everything he puts in print has to be reviewed by the NASD. Not only do they charge for this "service" but by the time they respond and approve the advertisement, the idea is obsolete. Who loses? The people who wanted to know about the opportunities, that's who.

You may not realize that your broker is not allowed to swap you from one family of mutual fund to another without having you sign a form indicating you are aware of the consequences—namely that you'll have to pay another commission. Is Big Brother trying to protect you from the unscrupulous practice of churning mutual funds? Sure. You pay around two percent to buy a stock and another two to sell it. Less if you buy on volume. Big Brother has no problem. You pay four percent or so to buy a front load mutual fund and nothing to sell it. Big problem! Does Big Brother make you sign a form to sell the stock? What's the difference? Who loses? You, the client—when your broker doesn't bother to call you to recommend the very same mutual fund swap that she may be doing in her own account. It's too much trouble. Big Brother has a problem with it.

Some of the requirements that come through would be comical if they weren't so serious. It's amazing what bureaucrats can dream up in the feeble attempt to justify their existence and render the term "buyer beware" totally obsolete. These problems are probably not so different in other industries but they have become acute in the brokerage industry and as a client, you should have a concept of how they affect you—and your profits.

Your broker is a little paranoid these days. He has to be. If he should refuse to do a transaction for you, or if he doesn't communicate in writing with you as much as he used to, don't jump to blame him. Understand the regulations, rules, policies and edicts that he is forced to work with, in his never ending attempt to balance the performance of your account with the restrictions he must endure.

Competition and Consolidation —The Banks.

22

Competition and Consolidation.
—The Banks

Competition is always fierce in any industry. The securities industry is no different. Your broker faces competition for your business from other firms. This, of course, is not in your worst interest. If your broker can't compete he probably shouldn't be your broker. But there should at least, be a level playing field. If your broker is over regulated and his competition is not, then he and his clients suffer.

One of the current competitive trends is the competition developing between brokerage houses and banks. As each begin to take on the others roles you may want to consider how it affects you.

Banks now compete for your investment dollars. Their original investment options, CD's and money markets, lost their luster as interest rates fell during the early 90's. By early 1994, bank tellers were shuffling customers over to the "investment desk" at record rates. The investment desk could offer better returns. A survey soon discovered that a significant majority of these bank customers were under the impression that the stock and bond mutual funds they bought, were guaranteed by the same federal agencies that insured their bank deposits. Not so, of course.

Had these customers purchased the funds through an investment broker, they would have undoubtedly known otherwise. By regulation and simply because of ethic, the investment brokers would have informed these customers of the risks they were taking. The banks made the commissions and the brokers didn't. It wasn't a level playing field. The banks didn't have the same regulators.

Why are banks now in the brokerage business? A brief history of recent banking is necessary in order to answer this question.

People always liked the bank CD's and money markets. They paid a decent return and were risk free, right? Well maybe.

They used to pay a decent return but those returns dropped rather dramatically and besides, they never were really risk free.

They were risk free to the *public* because Uncle Sam took on all of the risk by insuring them. The Federal Deposit Insurance Company (FDIC) and the Federal Savings and Loan Insurance Company (FSLIC) were the government agencies that were doing all of the insuring. If you loaned your money to the bank and it went broke, it was okay. Uncle would bail them out or give you back your money up to $100,000.

But who is the government? You, your friends and your neighbors, that's who. So who was doing the insuring? Anyone who paid federal taxes was assuming the risk of that insurance.

It got better. The banks were able to borrow money for paltry rates of return and their customers were happy to accept the low returns, because the loan was insured. The bank then went out and invested its money in higher paying investments, taking the spread on the difference. At first they invested mostly in mortgages. Uncle said he would insure the bank deposits so the banks could use the money to offer mortgages. Since the mortgages paid more than the banks borrowed the money for, they could make a few bucks in the process. Sounded fair enough.

Everybody would be able to get loans to buy houses and all would be fine in the world. It's called monitory intermediation. The bank was the mediator—the middle man in this respectable scenario. Uncle even limited how much interest the banks could pay out to depositors, to keep things on an even playing field.

Whoops. Inflation. Higher interest rates. T-bills paying more than the banks. Other investments were paying still more. Money moved out of the banks. "Disintermediation." No more bucks in the banks. No more mortgages. Housing crunch. Possible recession or depression in the offing.

Not to worry. Uncle can always fix the problem. Deregulation. Uncle takes off the limits on what the banks can pay out in interest. Banks can raise the rates on the money they borrow from their customers. Money pours back into the banks. Wrist watches. Toasters. Banks even give out money up front, if the customer gives them money to use for long periods of time. These longer term loans are called certificates of deposit. No more disintermediation, no more housing crunch. Sterling idea. Depression is aborted.

Hmmm. Banker number thirty six sits down and thinks about this whole thing for thirty seconds or so.

"If I can give my customers a higher rate than bankers one through thirty five I can get all of their depositors money. I can then invest it all and make more money. How can I do that? Invest the (depositors) money in higher paying, riskier loans. Joint ventures. Commercial real estate and junk bonds. That kind of stuff. My depositors won't care because Uncle is insuring them anyway! I'll make a fortune on the spread, borrowing money at, say six percent, and loaning it out at perhaps thirteen. Seven percent on a few billion dollars will definitely buy me a nice house, not to mention a secure retirement."

Bankers one through thirty five soon caught on. In order to compete with thirty six they had to play ball or they had to go out of business.

Recession. Commercial real estate folds. Junk bonds (originally an excellent investment concept for reasons we don't have time to go into here) get junkier, fold up and die. Banks can't pay up on all of those high yield CD's and guess what. Uncle's insurers, the FDIC and the FSLIC, go basically broke trying to bail them out. In order to prevent a complete collapse of the banking system the "Resolution Trust" is formed. Its purpose is to borrow money and bail out the banks so the FDIC and FSLIC won't have to—in other words, to pay off on all of those insured CD's.

Where did the money come from, for the Resolution Trust? They borrowed it of course, with bonds guaranteed by Uncle. Who guaranteed those bonds? Uncle's taxpayers, that's who.

Banks have historically performed a very valued service. They placed mortgages. They held pass book savings accounts. They offered checking accounts. They still do these things, but they like to make an extra buck or two in the process. Uncle really doesn't want the insurance risk on the deposits any more, so he has allowed the banks to offer investments. The banks make the commission dollars, adding to their solvency. These investments don't need to be insured. Uncle is happy.

Enter a new kind of broker. The bank broker. The banks simply hired brokers away from the brokerage companies. They pay the brokers less of a payout, but by pulling all of those people off of the CD lines, the bank brokers can make a few bucks. Actually they can make quite a bit more than a few bucks.

Make no mistake about it though. That bank investment broker has a quota he has to make. If it costs him a few lunches for the tellers, so they point customers in his direction, it's okay. The bank broker invests your money and it's on to the next person on line.

Did the brokerage houses stand idly by and watch this happen? Even before it did happen, the brokerage companies saw it coming. Enter the "management account." A full service brokerage account. Your investments, a sweep money market account (which automatically moves idle cash in and out of the money market, so it constantly earns interest), checks, a visa debit card to access the funds with, the works. All in one single account. It was a hot item. Brokers brought in millions of dollars of assets with it. People were literally lined up at the doors.

All of the major brokerage houses now have such accounts and they are very efficient. Just don't expect your broker to sit with you every week to reconcile your checkbook. He's not a banker and he doesn't get paid for that.

The money that the bank broker invests for you, doesn't go into the bank's assets. The commission dollars do, but the principal doesn't. The bank can't reinvest it, and make a profit on the spread.

It's still a bit uncertain as to what happens when the banks have no more deposit money because they've placed it all into mutual funds and annuities. Best betting, however, goes to a complete consolidation of the financial industry. Banks buy the brokerages. Brokerages buy the banks. They each become "financial centers."

You as a client, then get three choices.

First, you will be able to go to the financial center with the historical banking philosophy. All of your financial needs are fulfilled by this company. You get a different cashier each time you visit, and different specialists. You might never get the same person twice but someone will always there for what ever your needs. The second choice will have you going to the financial center that evolved from the brokerage company. Here, you still have one advisor (the ex-broker) all of the time. But now he is a generalist, probably working on salary. He can take care of most of your needs. If he can't, he performs the role of coordinator, obtaining the required specialist who can.

Third choice? You go to the independent advisor. Remember him. He is now truly the "corner deli" of this new financial investment world. Maximum service. You get individual attention by the boss. If you delight in ultimate personal service, this will be your guy. If you need a service he doesn't provide, however, you will be going to one of the other centers, or to another independent specialist who provides the service required.

Obtaining financial advice in the future will probably be just like obtaining legal advice today. Do you go to your independent lawyer or to a large law firm? There are advantages to either and in the investment world, doing business this way just might not be such a bad thing. What is the time frame for all of this? I think within ten years, at the latest.

Competition and consolidation are definitely happening in the securities business. Your broker is now busy figuring out just where he and his clients are going to fit in to all of this. As a client, you might also want to give it some thought.

Managed Money and Fees.

23

Managed Money and Fees

Money Management is definitely happening in the investment business. It's happening right now and it's happening big time. It will be growing. When you place your money with a money manager, you elect to give up control of the day to day investment decisions. You allow your manager to make these decisions for you, and for those expert decisions, you pay a fee.

There are currently three basic forms of managed money programs available to the average investor. The first is mutual fund managed money.

We have already discussed mutual funds in considerable detail. You give your money to the fund manager together with many other people, and they manage it for you. What is important to recognize here, is that the mutual funds are merely part of the larger trend—that of managed money.

We also touched on the second form of managed money, the "wrap account," when we talked about specialist brokers. Lets look at it a little more closely now and see how it developed.

Not unlike the mutual fund manager, the wrap fee money manager manages large sums of money. Today's largely successful wrap fee managers got their start in, and often continue to manage, large pension accounts or the assets of very substantial investors. One might have to commit sums in excess of a million dollars for one of these professionals to handle an account.

Until recently, these managers simply weren't interested in "small potatoes". It didn't pay. But then they started looking around. They looked at the brokerage companies and the billions of dollars of "little bucky's" (smaller accounts) that the brokerages controlled.

The brokerage house had the billions of little buckys but in order to make any money off these billions, the money has to keep generating commission dollars. Commissions depend on the whims of the market. Commissions are not a very stable source of income. The brokerages looked over their shoulders at the money managers. These guys don't get paid by commission. They get paid by fee. "Want me to manage your dollars? Pay me one percent of the dollars I manage whether I take them up, down or sideways."

The two kept eying each other's business and finally, a dialogue opened up.
BROKERS:

Hmmmm. "Can we talk for a few minutes here? I've got billions that I'd rather get paid a fee for."
MONEY MANAGERS:

"Really? I'd love another billion or two. I've got my own problems though. Those commissions you charge me to trade my accounts are pretty heavy."
BROKERS:

"Tell 'ya what. If I give you a billion or two in small accounts can you manage it with your big bucks? I'll charge you next to nothing for your street trades. You take your one percent, I'll take another two and give you the trades free.
MONEY MANAGERS, to themselves:

"Hmmmm. Two to five billion in new money. One percent, cheap trades. Interesting.

BROKERS, to themselves:

"Wow. Two percent on my itty bitty billions. I pay a couple of guys a salary to execute trades on the floor of the exchange and this guy manages all the money. If my clients don't like him we fire him and move on to the next guy. Not bad!"

TOGETHER, in unanimous harmony:

"Works for me."

"Works for me too."

Enter the birth of the wrap account. For an annual fee of around three percent of the assets you invest (usually deducted on a quarterly basis from your account) you get some of the top money managers in the country—perhaps the world. For your three percent you don't pay any trade commissions. The broker finds you a manager to your liking and off you all go into the sunset. You receive the same statement you would from your normal brokerage account, complete with a listing of transactions. You receive the same confirmations you normally would, reflecting what the manager buys and sells for you. No commissions, only that little wrap fee debit to your account once a quarter. You can buy this program for as little as a hundred thousand (in some cases fifty thousand) and your money is being managed by the same people as the big guys.

The battle rages on between brokers, their employers and their clients as to which of these two managed money programs is a better one. Suffice it to say that your broker gets paid either way. In the funds he gets paid more up front. With the wrap fee he gets paid more evenly over time, building an annuity for the future to sort of smooth out his income.

Wrap fee accounts are great cocktail hour conversation for clients.

"Well actually, *I* have a *money manager* handling my investments!"

"Gee! Wow—*really?*"

Of course you might want to give a little thought to the fact that your money manager—the one actually doing the work for you, is getting around a third of the fee you're paying. Interesting!

Performance varies between mutual funds and wrap fee managers. In either event your broker remains your main interface, continuing to watch market events and advise you on the performance of your account.

You can always change a fund. You can always fire a wrap fee manager. The three percent annual fee of the wrap program (slightly less for larger accounts) seems like an awful lot of money to some. On the other hand if you need to take losses at the end of the year for tax reasons, you can't exactly call your local mutual fund and tell them to sell you out of ABC and DEF shares at the loss. You can under the wrap fee program.

The bottom line is just that. Bottom line performance. After all of the fees are deducted, who made you more money?

The final concept in managed money is probably the most popular idea with both clients and brokers. The "broker-advisor." We mentioned this concept when we talked about the independent.

In this program, your broker takes on the function of money manager for your account. He forfeits commissions and acts as a fee based money manager. You no longer pay your broker by commission. Instead you pay him a fee of perhaps one or two percent of the assets. He then invests your money in the best, most efficient investments he can find. You don't have to ask yourself each time he calls, if he's simply looking for another commission. Unlike the fund or the wrap fee manager, it's *very* personal. You call him just like you do now. Any time you want to. He has discretion over your account so he can change the investments around whenever he has to. He gets the same pay though, whether he actively trades your account or he doesn't. You measure him like you do now, by performance. The difference is that you measure him as you would any other money manager, by performance of the entire account, not his last single idea.

The advantage to you and the broker? Your broker doesn't have to take time calling you if he sees an opportunity that needs to be acted on quickly. In effect, you become a "do it" client. Your broker is never influenced by commission dollars earned. More importantly, *neither are you.* Clients miss *countless* investment opportunities because they are unwilling to pay commissions. Personal service by your own personal money manager. Sounds nice, doesn't it?

Perhaps, but some would argue that it doesn't quite work that way. Since your broker is getting paid whether he actively manages the account or not, he has far less incentive to constantly monitor the account as he should. There is nothing like the transaction based business (commissions paid on each transaction) to keep your broker alert to your account. He is constantly screening his accounts for any opportunity that will allow him to earn his next commission. Hopefully, if you have a good broker, the next transaction truly is a good one for you and not simply a "commission swap idea" (an idea on how to change the investments with the primary concern being to obtain a commission).

It would be nice if we all had a choice but there's a problem. Most large brokerage companies are simply not allowing this service. Remember, brokerage companies don't measure your broker's performance by the value he is able to add to your account. They measure his performance by commissions he earns his company. The companies are quite concerned with the idea of allowing their brokers, who are still primarily considered sales people, to actually manage client money. Are they trained? Are they capable of doing it?

It's a fair question. If your broker is an intellect, a specialist or an investment consultant, he is probably more than capable of managing your money—and coincidentally would produce more revenue for the firm if he were allowed to. Remember, these brokers spend a lot more time researching and managing accounts than they do prospecting for new clients. Conversely, if your broker's focus is more towards the sales side of the business, he may not be the capable money manager you would really need. And how would the brokerage company be able to discriminate between them? How would they even begin such a program?

At the present time, if your broker wishes to provide you with the broker-advisor option, he probably has to transfer to a smaller company that allows such services or become an independent on his own. This often means giving up the support that he receives from his larger company and many brokers are not ready to make such a dramatic change. Many clients would also hesitate leaving the security of the larger firm.

The concept is alive and growing, however. Many brokers have already been forced to make the move to smaller companies or have simply gone independent. They need to be able to provide these services to clients, who are more and more frequently, requesting them. The larger brokerage companies will eventually have to come to grips with the issue.

Until they do, you have a choice. You can stay with your favorite commission broker at his large brokerage company, or you can opt for the lesser known companies or the independents that *can* offer you the broker-advisor service.

Ideas that are working for Smart Investors.

24

Ideas that are working for Smart Investors.

I couldn't leave you, without first sharing some ideas that are currently working for smart investors. They are not terribly unique ideas. I didn't invent them and many of you may already be aware of them. But they often work and they *are* worth reviewing.

I'm also not offering these thoughts as specific recommendations to you. (Time for a legal disclaimer here!) To many financial writers are willing to offer financial advice to mass markets without the slightest concern for the investor's individual circumstance. I am not one of them. I am not your financial advisor and only he or she knows your individual situation well enough to make specific recommendations. These are, however, general ideas you may wish to explore in greater detail—concepts that have worked and continue to work for investors who are in the right position to take advantage of them.

I'm also not going to get to technical on you. My objective is to introduce you to the concept and let you review the technical aspects with your broker should you wish to.

BOND SWAPS

As we now know, bonds rise and fall in value over the life of their maturity. While we primarily purchase them to produce consistent income and with the intent of holding them for extended periods of time, occasionally unique opportunities arise. Smart investors take advantage of unique opportunities.

If interest rates have risen dramatically since you purchased your long term bonds, the value of your bonds has fallen. You may be showing significant paper losses (losses that you have in your account but that are not recognizable for tax purposes because you haven't sold the bonds). If you sell the bonds, you recognize the tax loss but then you have no bonds to pay you your income. A bond swap can give you the best of both worlds. You simply sell the bonds you own and buy similar bonds in the same market. In order to qualify for the tax loss you must meet the common "two out of three" rule. The bonds you purchase must be different from the bonds you sold in two out of the three following criteria:

1. The bonds purchased must be from a different issuer.
2. The bonds purchased must offer a different coupon rate.
3. The bonds purchased must have a different maturity date.

Play it safe and go for three out of three. By doing this, you will have in effect, swapped four quarters for a dollar bill. You still have bonds that are providing you with income but now you have a tax loss. This loss can offset any capital gains you may have. Up to three thousand dollars of losses per year (above any capital gains) can be a deduction against ordinary income. If you have more than three thousand dollars against income, the losses can be carried forward to future years until used up by offsetting future capital gains or until the three thousand dollars per year is used up.

Smart investors have saved lots of tax dollars by using this technique—if and when it's appropriate.

Another bond swap used particularly in the municipal or tax free markets, is the "Pre-refunded" or "Short Maturity" swap. You may own bonds that were originally purchased as longer term bonds. Usually, not always, the yield to maturity is higher on these longer term bonds. As time goes on, the "term" of these bonds naturally gets shorter— and the bonds trade at the value of shorter term bonds. This fact may not jump right out off your statement and slap you in the face, because most statements reflect the "current yield" of the bond, that is, the yield of its coupon rate divided by its current price. This may be much higher than the actual yield to maturity.

Many bonds also have what is known as a "call" feature. The issuer is allowed to call the bonds away from you (give you back your money and take back the bonds) at a date earlier than the stated maturity. When interest rates drop, you can bet your issuer is going to call the bonds. Why should he keep borrowing at a higher rate? Often, the issuers "Pre-refund" the bonds. They issue new bonds at a lower rate and with the proceeds, purchase treasury bonds as collateral against the original ones. You don't have to know all of the mechanics but what you should know is that these bonds will definitely be called at the earliest possible date. They too, begin trading as shorter term bonds.

If your objective is still to hold longer term bonds, (and earn the equivalent higher yield to maturity) you no longer are. In addition, if you have profits in the bonds you may find that the current market is valuing them at a greater price than they will be called at. Put another way, you are holding bonds that have a "guaranteed loss" built into them.

If you have such bonds, the current yield that you see on your statement is deceiving because it doesn't factor in this guaranteed loss. The actual yield to maturity (the yield that factors in the guaranteed reduction in the value of the bonds) may be considerably less. The "red light" to look for on your statement is the description "Pre-refunded." You may benefit from selling these bonds and purchasing other ones with a longer life span. If you have any questions, you should either do the math or contact your financial advisor for advice.

SYSTEMATIC WITHDRAWAL FOR INCOME

In today's current low interest rate environment, many investors are finding it difficult to obtain the income they either need or desire, by simply buying or owning bonds. Yields on quality bonds are low and even on the lower quality (junk) bonds, the returns are not very attractive to many. In addition, unless we are re-investing part of the income, we have virtually no chance for growth. We are not going to be *increasing* our income *or* principal if we are in bonds, money markets or CD's and are spending all of the income we currently receive. We need to do this to fight inflation. Our groceries are probably going to cost us more in the future.

It is not terribly difficult, however, to locate quality stock funds that have consistently returned in excess of ten percent over time. This may not mean they gained ten percent in every year, but on the average they have done so. Many in fact, have returned considerably more. Stock funds usually don't pay much of a dividend. Their returns come primarily from gains or, put another way, from the increase in their share value. Does it matter? If you're up twenty percent, it really doesn't matter whether it's from dividends or growth. You're still up twenty percent. We also can't guarantee future performance from past performance but a good long term track record is certainly going to suggest a continuing good future track record. So what do we do?

Lets say we have one hundred thousand dollars in bonds or CD's currently earning us five percent. That's five thousand dollars to live off of, not counting taxes. We go shopping. We find a mutual stock fund that has averaged fifteen percent returns over the last ten years. Not a bad track record. We buy the fund and tell them that each month, we want them to sell whatever amount of shares it takes, to pay us eight hundred thirty three dollars. That's right. Just send us the check. They will. Automatically.

Eight hundred thirty three dollars each month is ten thousand dollars a year. On the one hundred thousand, it's ten percent!

The fund then proceeds to have its average year and is up by fifteen percent. We only took out ten. We now have a new balance in the fund of one hundred five thousand dollars (the five thousand additional dollars being the five percent that we didn't take out, from the total return of fifteen. Not bad. At ten percent, we can now take out eight hundred seventy five dollars a month. Our principal grew, but so did our income.

This keeps on going until the fund has a really bad year. If it returns ten percent in the bad year we don't care. We broke even. If it returns less, we either take less per month, or take the same and wait for the better years. If we get nervous about the stock market from time to time, we simply go back and look equity performance over the last ten years or so. We look at the crash of '87 and the mini crash of '90. We look at how stocks recovered and how they have since grown. Then we cash our checks and go back to sleep. The investor that the bank told to "sleep tight—don't worry" is now up at two o'clock in the morning biting her nails, trying to figure out how to pay the next rent check.

Your broker or financial advisor should be able to provide you with what is called a "hypothetical" report showing the returns that your or her favorite stock mutual fund would have actually provided over past periods. (If she can't, go find another broker.) You'll probably be amazed at what your money could have been doing for you. In any event, if you need or desire more income than you are currently getting, you have to ask yourself a question. Would you rather get it from junk bonds—or high quality stocks?

ANCHOR STOCKS WITH ZERO'S

"Neither a borrower or a lender be." Shakespeare, *Hamlet*, 1, 3. And here you are lending your money to banks, municipalities, corporations or maybe even the U.S. Government in the form of money markets, CD's, bonds or treasuries while you could be "owning America." Well, maybe The Bard was right but the idea of putting so much of your money into stocks still scares the hoobies out of you. "Oh well." You can't "have your cake and eat it too", can you? Well, no—but you *almost* can.

Zero coupon bonds are just that. Bonds. Like any other bond the issuer guarantees their maturity and if the issuer happens to be the United States Government that guarantee is pretty secure. Okay! I hear the chuckles out there but hey, your lending your money out anyway, right? Zero coupon bonds don't pay dividends. They don't send you checks to buy goodies for the grandchildren with. You buy them at what is called a "discount" and they mature to full face value. Let's put that in English. You might buy bonds that in fifteen years, will mature to one hundred thousand dollars. It may cost you about forty thousand for those bonds. The actual numbers vary from day to day because they are bonds and like any bond they are priced according to current interest rates, but that's the general concept.

Your broker can get more specific when you're ready, but lets use these numbers for now.

You have the hundred thousand. You're worried about stocks going down and about the possibility of losing you your principal. If you buy the zero's for forty thousand you are guaranteed to have your one hundred thousand back in fifteen years. If you place the balance of sixty thousand into quality stocks *and lose all of it,* you are still going to have the principal back in fifteen years. Of course if you lost all of the money in stocks right away, you would have no income to live off of for that fifteen years—but if your sixty is in two or three quality mutual stock funds and that happens, we're probably *all* on the bread lines. Those loans you're now holding probably won't be worth much either!

Buy the way, if that sixty thousand is in systematic withdrawal plans at ten percent, that's six thousand a year or about six percent of the original hundred—with still plenty of potential for growth.

BI-HI!

Lets talk about those of us who like to buy and sell stocks—individual pieces of ownership in the corporations of America. This philosophy works for stock funds too, but lets talk stocks.

Conventional wisdom. Buy them low and sell them high. Why not try a different approach. Buy them high and sell them higher! If I'm at the railroad station getting on a train, I want the train to be going in the direction I want to go in, not in the other direction! If I want to buy a stock, don't I want the same thing? The concept is not new. In financial circles it is known as "momentum investing." You buy stocks that are going in the direction you want them to go in (up) and you buy the ones that are already doing it—with momentum.

Lets think about this in another way. Do you want to buy stocks that everybody else wants to own and are being bought? Or would you prefer to own stocks that no one else wants to own and are being sold off? I'm not suggesting that there aren't opportunities for "bottom fishing" the market (buying stocks at their lows) but the risk of them going lower, or at best staying flat for longer than you want to think about, are severe. It takes at the least, a pretty good market technician (stock chartist) to pick out the ones that are ready to swing back up and even *they* are wrong—lots of the time.

The discipline of buying high may sound simple but it takes a lot of courage to implement it. Why?

"It's up so high. It has to come down, doesn't it?"

Sure. When it's ready to, we'll sell it.

"How will I know when it's ready to come down?"

We'll get to that. For now lets look for some of the simpler buy signals.

The stock is making a new high. It has never been at this high price before. *Something* must be going right. Check out everything else you want to know about the stock before you buy it (recent news, its fundamental situation, perhaps the trends of the industry it's in) but the fact that it just reached a new high and has maybe been doing so for a few days, *isn't usually a bad thing*. You may just want to buy it.

The stock had a long term down trend but recently it has started coming back up. It's now at thirty and you wish you could have bought it at twenty five, its lows. Still, you like it and it looks like it could go higher. Is it just a false start? Take a look at the price action back when it was going down. Look for periods that it stopped going down and stayed flat for awhile—or maybe even went back up a little. These periods are what was called "support" in the price of the stock. They are price points when buyers came in and supported the price at that level. But the stock didn't make it. The buyers who bought it there were the "bottom fishers" who thought they were buying at the low, but they were wrong and the stock, after a few false starts, dropped further. That old support level (or price) is now a "resistance level" for the stock. A lot of people are going to want to sell the stock at that price and at least break even on their original purchase. If the stock is now going up, it could continue to go up or it could drop back and go down further just like it did back then. If, on the other hand, it "breaks through" that resistance it really does have at least some significant momentum to the upside and most likely will move forward to its next level of resistance. You might want to wait until it breaks through that level. You're buying high, but your buying a stronger stock and you're buying it with a lot more confidence.

Anybody can buy a stock. The hard part is selling it. You bought the stock. It worked. It's still going up. You have two choices now. You can hold it for the long term knowing it will go up and down from time to time, or you can look for an opportunity to sell it, thereby increasing your profit and reducing your risk that it will go down a lot more than you expected it to. You decide that you really like the stock but you would rather minimize your risk. The stock stops going up or perhaps starts going up at a much slower rate than it has been. Barring any unusual negative news events that cause it to drop sharply, it will probably flatten out for awhile, staying at about the same price for a period of time. It has found a new "resistance level." It may go up from here, or it may go back down.

You may want to familiarize yourself with some basic

chart techniques here (or a broker who knows his charts) to fine-tune your decision. Moving Average Convergence Divergence indicators, Stochastics and trend channels are but a few of many the technical tools used to define the sell point but one thing should be clear even without them. If the stock starts going down again, you have risk. You don't know where it will end up. If you sell it here, you have profits. The worst that can happen is that it starts to go up again and you don't own it. You can always buy it back and there are always other stocks going up. Certainly, if it goes down below its prior resistance level (now its support level) *lose it*. And wait until it reaches its old high again before you buy it back. It might take a lot longer than you thought.

Buying high. Oh, so easy to talk about—and oh, so hard to do. But smart investors do it all the time.

Here are a few more thoughts.

Never own a security you wouldn't want to buy more of. If you wouldn't want to buy it, chances are others don't either. Sell it and wait for the sentiment (yours and others) to change.

Take losses. If you have a security that has performed poorly, sell it. Don't think of it as a loss. Don't spend your time worrying about the gains or losses of an individual security. Concentrate instead, on the gain or loss of the entire portfolio.

Your money is a finite resource. Whether a single investment is up or down is immaterial. You want the total of that finite resource working as hard as it can for you, at any given time.

Never marry an investment. Save your emotions for your spouse, your significant other, your sports utility vehicle or some other object worthy of your love and adoration. Far too many people have held on to their favorite stock as it sunk to unthinkable lows, simply because they "loved" the company. Buy a stock you hate once in awhile (as long as it's going up), just to teach yourself some discipline.

Fundamental investing is the science of reviewing stocks based on their earnings, their balance sheets, their management and overall financial strength. Technical investing is the art of analyzing the price movement of the stock. Fundamental investing tells you whether or not *you* like the stock. Technical investing tries to tell you whether *others* like the stock. Use both—or find a who broker does. Fundamentals tell you that you want to *own* the stock. Technical tell you *when* you want to own it.

Don't judge stock mutual funds based on a magazine or newspaper's report of those that have recently (perhaps finally) had their "day in the sun"—especially if the fund happens to be advertising in the magazine or newspaper and contributing to their revenues. Look for *long term performance.* Judge stock mutual funds not only on their returns, but also the *risks they took* to obtain them. Consult an independent mutual fund rating service or consult a broker who has access to one. You want *maximum performance* with *minimum risk.* Nothing less.

I have to go now. As I close this chapter the market is once again, flirting with new highs—and there are some stocks *I really want to buy!*

In Summary.

25

In Summary

The relationship with a stock broker is a personal one. Any personal relationship becomes more rewarding when each of the parties understand where the other is coming from. What makes the person "tick?" What are the concerns, the issues he faces?

We have discussed why you may need the services of a stock broker, and the services he provides. We have talked about who he is, how he operates and what tools he has to operate with.

We now know, or at least know to ask, who he works for. We have a basic knowledge not only of how he makes his money, but how much money he actually makes. We have also explored what type of stock broker he is, and also the different types of clients he works for. In the process, we have explored how we, as clients, may become *better* clients, thus reaping the benefits of a better broker-client relationship. We know about some of the issues that concern him, from the size of his book and how it affects him, to changes taking place in his industry and how they are affecting not only him, but his clients.

We know quite a bit more about the laws he operates under and how regulation is restricting not only his business, but the recommendations he can make to his clients.

We have a better idea as to why he might change companies, and also how we might be affected when he does. We know how to handle the "distribution process," when our account is arbitrarily and very definitely *with* prejudice, assigned to another broker we know nothing about.

If we are novice investors, we have learned some of the fundamentals of investing. Not only have we learned what basic types of investments there are but we have also explored different ways to invest in the investments that may interest us.

We have also learned that to your investment broker, information is power. Information and knowledge allow him to make the informed decisions that will make his clients money. Information is the power that will allow him to take money from other people and put it where it belongs, in his "book." And we know by now of course, that when he places profits in his book, he is in fact, placing them in his clients' accounts.

The information *you* now possess, is also power! Use it well.

Use it in selecting investments that you are most comfortable with, now that you understand the different risks and rewards.

Use it to select the right broker for you. Or use it to enhance the relationship with the broker you now have.

Use your new found power to alert you to the potential pitfalls of investing. Use it, together with your broker, in developing investment strategies that work best for you— not somebody else, but *you*.

Use your newly found power to plot your investment strategy in a changing investment world. Who do you want to deal with in the future? The investment center or the independent? Who will your broker be working for in the future? Are you going to be comfortable with his choice? Use your new found power to understand why your broker makes a recommendation to you, or why he doesn't.

As we invest in the present, and as the future unfolds, may you and your stock broker realize good fortune, good profit, and the ultimate in investment success.

To Contact the Author—

Francis W. Miller
P.O. Box 497
Port Jefferson, NY 11777-0497
E Mail: WareF@AOL.com